ISBN: 978-1-937543-92-1

Published by Jaded Ibis Press, *sustainable literature by digital means*™ an imprint of Jaded Ibis Productions, LLC, Seattle, Washington USA.

Cover and interior design by Debra Di Blasi. Book editing by Elizabeth J. Colen. Photographs from the personal collection of Amanda Montei.

This book is available in multiple formats. Visit our website for more information: jadedibisproductions.com

Two Memoirs

An Auto+Biography

Amanda Montei

Jaded Ibis Press
sustainable literature by digital means™
an imprint of Jaded Ibis Productions
SEATTLE • HONG KONG • BOSTON

I believe that always, or almost always, in all childhood and in all the lives that follow them, the mother represents madness. Our mothers always remain the strangest, craziest people we've ever met.

—Marguerite Duras

People who need people/
Are the luckiest people in the world.

—Barbra Streisand

PART ONE

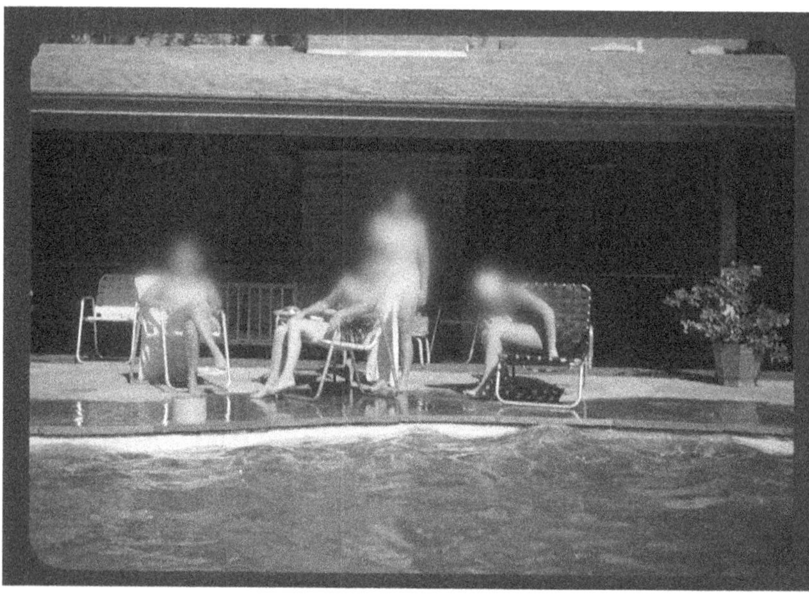

amanda MONTEI

THE HOLLYWOOD HILLS HOUSE

This is the truth. I hope.

I should start with the first memory.[1]

I am pushing a vacuum, I think. My parents started me on the vacuum early. I am waddle-young. Fat-face little towhead. I'm pushing my plastic vacuum but I probably do not understand why I have been given a vacuum to play with since our live-in housekeeper, Teresa, does all the work around the house. My mother doesn't do that sort of thing. She's much too busy. So I am likely imagining that I am the housekeeper. Though it occurred several years later, years after the divorce, next to this vacuuming memory is the memory of me holding a bobby pin to a door lock. I am pretending the bobby pin is a key. I am a working woman coming home from a long day, fiddling with the lock, exasperated, just like my mother. I also cook in my play kitchen, which has a microwave and a stove that looks like its metal coils are always burning hot. It has a little plastic refrigerator too, in which I keep plastic fruit, a plastic steak, and a plastic bottle of milk. The plastic food makes me salivate.

Then: I am standing naked in the foyer of our big Hollywood Hills House. I am crying and I am small. I have thrown my dress up in the air and it is now caught on the chandelier. Why did I throw my dress up in the air? In exultation. In anger. For attention. The chain of events is lost to me. The dress is burning, hard up against the light

---

1 She would say it's hard to know where to begin, hard to know where a life begins. Life just isn't that way. Her mother made her promise before she died that she would tell her story. Or maybe she said our story. It's important to know where things went wrong, how things got so ugly. How she got so ugly. She would say there is so much I can't know. After all, I was only a girl, and everyone tries to hide the truth from little girls.

bulb, a special bulb that looks like a candle flame. My older sister, Melissa, is beside me, comforting me. Teresa assesses the situation. Her skin is so smooth. She goes at the dress with a broom, standing at the top of the stairs so she can reach the chandelier. I wait below in the foyer, my arms open wide like *I love you this much.* I wait for my burning dress to return to me. Melissa, four years older, is beside me in a dress that matches my burning dress. She is also wearing soft old-fashioned gloves with lace-trim. She is holding me, hugging me, saying it will be okay. My dress will return soon.[2]

My parents came home after lush parties, all fancied-up and wasted, and found Teresa crying, standing in that same foyer with her bags packed. Teresa slept in the garage, which was beside the pool in our backyard. My mother often misplaced her jewelry, and accused Teresa of stealing it. When my sister and I broke one of my mother's European-style brick houses, which she collected and set on the mantle, she blamed Teresa. But my mother was not why Teresa threatened to leave. The closest she came was the night I had a sleepover with the daughter of a CBS news anchor who was well known for greeting all of Southern California from the desert to the sea. My sister was slumber partying elsewhere, and we thought it might be fun to let Melissa's bunny rabbit Bunnicula ride headfirst down my bunkbed ladder, sort of like a bumpy slide. The rabbit seemed to enjoy the game, so we let it ride down again and again.

Bunnicula grew tired suddenly. We tucked her in for the night in my Cabbage Patch play-crib.

When my parents came home Teresa said, "They're evil, Mrs. Elizabeth."

We buried Bunnicula in the backyard the next morning. My

---

2 She would say her first memory is of her grandfather leaving her, while she was going to the bathroom. Her grandfather died before she was born, so she never knew him. He was always with her though, until one day, when she was sitting on the toilet, he told her that she was getting too old to have a ghost like him hanging around. He had to leave her for good.

father dug a small hole in the dirt patch by the pool, and I took the bunny out of the box and draped her on my shoulders. My mother wore fur this way. She was on the balcony and caught me doing this, saw me dancing around and humming, my eyes on the brush below us, on the skyline of Los Angeles below the hills. My mother tried to punish me, to keep me away from play dates, but she had no follow through.

I often demanded Teresa cook me *queso en plato.* Melted cheese on a plate.

Then Teresa wrapped my hips with my mother's green scarves and we played *The Little Mermaid.* I told Teresa she had to play the ugly, evil octopus.[3]

When my parents left the house in fur and leather, I cried against Teresa. I did this the night my parents left for the Grammys, the year before they divorced. Did I know it was the last time my mother would be dressed this way? My father was already walking to our

---

3 As girls, my mother and her twin sister Melissa spent afternoons driving up and down the immaculate streets of Hancock Park in their red surrey with the fringe top. The lawns sloped up and around them, spilling onto stately porches with huge front doors. Though they were fraternal twins, they looked nearly identical. They had the same soft pout, the same scraggly hair. They could only pick themselves out in childhood pictures if they were wearing their Twin A and Twin B shirts, which they wore until they left home.

Weekends in The Big Brick French Normandy in Hancock Park were spent watching my mother's older sister leap off the backyard diving board with pointed toes, and enter splashless into the Olympic-sized pool. My mother and her sisters' swimming caps had red fringe, too. Their older brother made regular appearances on *Ozzie and Harriet* and *Dobie Gillis*. Their father produced a television show about a callous bank president named Cosmo Topper. Topper was haunted by two old clients, who had died in an avalanche. The clients, a well-to-do married couple, had been vacationing in a snowy locale with their St. Bernard and the dog died with them, so of course he also haunted Topper. The dog wore a barrel under his neck all the time, and my mother's parents told her this barrel held "spirits." She supposed ghosts could fit themselves into just about anything, even such a small barrel, but didn't understand why they traveled this way. Topper's own ghosts—the Kirbys—were very well dressed, and they brought much needed excitement into old Topper's life.

brand-new silver Volvo station wagon when my mother promised to bring me home something *exquisite* to eat. After she divorced my father, the scene was the same, but she left alone or with a man I didn't know, and I cried against a doorjamb.

That night my mother returned bathed in light, with stories about who they had seen at the award show. She brought me a Styrofoam box with crispy duck inside, the skin fried and sweet, and I ate it up. She said, "You have such refined taste buds." I told everyone at school.

Before my parents divorced, my mother and father owned a studio on Sunset Boulevard, where they managed fledgling musicians and produced records. My father,[4] whose early music career had failed,

---

4 If we forget the ugliness of her teenage years, she would say her troubles started with my father. He never changed a diaper, never bought her anything nice, never did the laundry, and still never felt she was doing enough for him. But she would admit that he was once an amazing guitar player. She would admit there was once just a boy and a girl who loved each other.

She met him in 1969, the summer of love and the summer before she began ninth grade. She never forgot the first time he showed up on her lawn in Hancock Park, perched on his Sting-Ray bike with the banana seat. (She had a vision of my sister's freckled face, her dark curly hair, when he rode off that day.) He was still rail-thin, with awkward buckteeth and long black hair. She thought he was edgy.

He dated her twin sister first. Melissa was always hipper than she was, always attracted boys. She was never certain whether or not my father and Melissa kissed, but their brief relationship became one of those mythological things, something that loomed over my parents' marriage. The three of them smoked pot together in his little Honda after school. When Melissa refused to go to a Blood, Sweat and Tears concert with my father, he took my mother instead, and this was when they first kissed.

She must have been reading something romantic at the time. Reading books had become a way to escape. Life had turned ugly at home after her father lost his job. They had moved to The Apartment on Irving Drive, which was still in Hancock Park, but was the size of the living room in The Big Brick French Normandy.

A few weeks after the concert, they went to the beach with their friend Jodie, who he had felt up. They sat in the sand with their backs together and their knees up when my mother began to get seductive, batting her

convinced my mother to start this business with him, and after investing money given to them by both of their parents, they made enough to put us up in the Hollywood Hills. In my mind's eye, I am always dressed in a white and gold dress with a lace collar in that house. My sister is in her favorite dress too: a red velvet one, also with a lace collar.

My sister and I each had copies of each other's favorite dresses, because for every special occasion we ordered corresponding outfits out of a catalogue that specialized in that kind of thing. We were matching, laced-collared people then. We took trips to Hawaii every summer, and my sister and I posed in front of the camera in matching pink muumuus, matching pink sunburns. My mother called me Moo Moo, and my sister and I wondered if I had been nicked-named after the dress or the cow sound. We flew first-class and on my first airplane ride, while sipping my free orange juice, I lay back and crossed my legs the way I had seen my mother do and I sighed deeply, happily.

"This is the life I've been waiting to want," I said. My mother laughed until my cheeks flushed. She told that story for years.

My mother always talked about her life as a series of houses, each with their own aura, their own sense of rebirth and subsequent abandonment. In turn, I too learned to serialize my life this way. At The Hollywood Hills House it felt like we had everything. A two-story house tucked in the windy, narrow roads above Sunset

---

eyes and pushing her breasts together. She knew she was manipulating him a little. She decided she would steal him from Melissa. She wanted him to love her. In the car that afternoon, after they got rid of Jodie, she told him everything about her family, about the horrible fighting. She wasn't sure that he cared, but he listened, and then he told her that his mother used to pay him to eat when he was young. He thought he might have issues with food because of it. He also told her he had a long lost brother, who his mother had left on a doorstep in New York before he was born. (No one ever found him.) She fell in love, or something like love. Soon they were spending weekends at Wallichs Music City on Sunset and Vine, test-driving 45s and kissing each other in those little soundproof rooms.

Boulevard. A foyer that stretched into a cordoned off kitchen, an expansive dining and living room—the downstairs space lined on one side with wall-high sliding glass doors that looked out on our pool, which had a mini zip-line running over it. My room and those windows had a view of the entire Los Angeles skyline. My mother used to say, "Don't you just *love* your view of the entire Los Angeles skyline?"[5]

My parents' room was something frightening then, something I was too young to experience. My parents, in a way, were like that too.

I don't remember where Melissa was on the nights they went out, though I'm sure we played together often. She was always watching over me, always coddling me. But I spent most of my free time with Teresa. I became very good at ordering her around. "Queso en plato, por favor," I would say, and snap my fingers. She would shred cheddar cheese onto my favorite mermaid plate and put it in the microwave. I sucked on the greasy cheddar pancake while watching my parent's laser disc of *Hard Day's Night*.

I worshipped my mother then: her long brown hair, her fancy dresses with shoulder pads, puffy lamé sleeves and cinched waists. The way she held her drinks at the parties they threw, when she still pretended to love my father. She draped her arm around me when I

---

5 Topper and his ghosts brought my grandparents to Los Angeles from New York. Topper helped pay for The Big Brick French Normandy in Hancock Park, the one with the Olympic-sized pool, and all the big houses before it. When my mother's parents invited photographers into their home, the family posed with Benny, the black man in the white suit who drove my grandfather to Samuel Goldwyn studios every morning, and with Macy, the black woman who cooked all the family meals. My mother always felt that Benny and Macy were part of the family. On the weekends, their home was host to soirees and whisky-ice-clinking evenings with Conrad Hilton, Ricky Nelson and the man who would eventually cancel *The Smothers Brothers*. Fancy couples moved about the living room, weightless, seamless. Starlets with furs and red lips drooping down loose happy faces, bodies hanging on the arms of chairs. My mother and her sister were called on to perform songs and skits, mix drinks, and then asked to get out of the way. "Children are to be seen and not heard," her mother would say.

ran up to her, even when she was talking away. Without pause, she picked olives off the broken marble slabs that Teresa carried around.

During the holidays, my mother put out place cards, and we entertained her twin sister Melissa and our cousins. I liked watching my mother choose everyone's seats and write in their names with her loopy calligraphic hand. I stuffed gold glitter napkins into brown seashell napkin holders.

She organized the silent auction and the yearly fair at Buckley, our private school, and enlisted the help of her friends, who were all rich and famous or married to rich and famous men. She was good friends with Tito Jackson's wife Dee Dee. They lunched regularly with a group of well-to-do women who also wore fancy dresses with shoulder pads, puffy lamé sleeves and cinched waists. At the last fair we attended, I won a goldfish in a sack race and was bit on the hand by a yappy Dachshund I was trying to pet. My mother came to me crying under her huge oversized glasses, red lips pursed. She rushed me into the car, hurrying my father and sister.

"Oh, the day is ruined," she must have said.[6]

---

6 She hated to think of herself as a high school dropout, but after leaving home, she quit high school and began running a needlepoint store on Fairfax between Santa Monica and Melrose, across from Genghis Cohen. In that little shop, everything was pre-planned and pre-determined. She knew she couldn't fuck anything up, so long as she worked carefully. If she counted her stitches and followed the pattern, something beautiful always emerged, and she found comfort in that. She saved up money with my father, who had started a band. She did most of the earning and saving. Then my father's father—a man who was always smiling with his deep set dimples—had a sudden heart attack and died.

They used the inheritance to put a down payment on a house in Simi Valley. When the bank told them they couldn't go through escrow because they were still under eighteen, my father called and pretended to be a lawyer, and the bank let them have their first home loan. She bought my father a bunny named Mr. Valentine. They walked into the living room weeks later to check on him and his entire head was gone. Severed. She thought later she should have taken it as some sort omen.

That year, one of the sisters found herself with an unwanted pregnancy and she had to terminate it. But the details of all that, she would say, should

I ran into a wall that same year when a boy, whom I would later marry on the schoolyard, challenged me to a race. We were supposed to run across the blacktop and touch the stucco wall, then turn around and run back to where we started. I was so determined not to let this boy win, to show him I had just as much in me as he had, that I just kept running right smack into that wall, and fell to the ground. I left school that day in a flurry with my mother, a round wound—all mottled and pricked from the grainy wall—on my forehead.

"One day you were sitting on my hip everywhere we went and then the next—" she used to say as she braided my hair before school. "I wish so badly I had realized at the time that I'd never hold you like that again." She stared sadly into my eyes often.[7] "I hope you never

---

not be shared with anyone outside the family. It was then that her parents realized they had to get their family together. My grandfather caved, agreed to use my grandmother's family money, which he had been too prideful to accept before. They bought The House in Bel Air, a fresh start. My grandfather got sober just like that, and never drank again. My grandmother was in hats and dresses again, like nothing had ever changed. Like The Apartment on Irving had never happened.

My mother was nineteen when she married my father. Her parents weren't happy about the wedding but you wouldn't have known it. They were tired of hating their daughter.

7 Even though the family moved on years later, pretended it all away, she would say that the years in The Apartment on Irving never left her." She ran away from home in the fall of 1972. The year Elton John came out with "Tiny Dancer," which was the one and only song my father (or any man) ever said made him think of her. She was seventeen.

They had been living in The Apartment for years, her father chasing after her every night, in his heavy wing tips. When she ran away she thought she would sleep over at my father's mother's condo in Hollywood, just off the 101, but as soon as her parents read her note that night, they called my father's mother and told her that they would be furious if she were to harbor their daughter. His mother said that she didn't want that kind of shit in her house. His mother was a big deal at the time, head of Beechwood Music. My mother had always admired her. She would go on to work as the Vice President of Capitol Records, the first woman to do so. Fred MacMurray had been the best man at my father's parents' wedding, and before their

grow to hate your mother," she said. I dreamt of being close to her all the time, forever, but of course I didn't tell her.[8]

My favorite friend at the time ate nothing but white food. White bread, white cheese, white peaches. Her father was a Duke of France and her mother was the sister of Mike Curb, of Curb Records, so she got away with that sort of thing. She wore mary janes and wide-brimmed hats to parties. The white food girl also took vacations to France regularly, and sometimes my parents went along with her family. They loaded up dark town cars with Louis Vuitton suitcases before dawn. My sister and I stayed in Los Angeles with Teresa. It was just too hard to cart us girls around Europe, my mother said.

At the white food girl's house, I cut bangs into my hair, determined to cover up the conspicuous scab that formed after I ran

---

divorce, they had regular parties with Fred, June Haver, Frank and Grace DeVol. This was a well-connected, single, working woman—very different from my mother's mother, who by then was already deeply depressed.

That night, my father rolled a couple of jays and drove my mother out to the back of the Hollywood Bowl parking lot and they smoked until they burnt their fingers. They talked a little about their futures, and then he waved goodnight and left her in his Honda, in that empty parking off Mulholland Drive. It was the time of the Hollywood Strangler, who was raping and killing young women right in the area where she now found herself alone and high. She would say my father never stayed in the car with her, not for one day. He never spent one night out of his cozy warm safe bed. The Honda was so small, barely big enough for her to sleep in the back seat much less another human, so in that sense, it was for the best. Years later, she found an old commercial online for the same little Honda. In the commercial, a man drives around town putting in smaller gas pumps and more parking meters since the Honda Sedan takes up such little space.

That's how it went every night until she found a place to stay. The joints helped her fall asleep but then the rain jet sprinklers would come on at two in the morning and they sounded like bullets. She jumped awake every time, and hugged herself until the sun came up again. Her parents knew where she was, but they never came to get her.

8 When she couldn't handle sleeping in the Honda anymore, she stayed with her only real friend, Bernie, sweet sweet Bernie. She would say that Bernie saved her life, and she wished years later, when Bernie was diagnosed with cancer, that she could have done the same for her.

into the wall. My mother was furious about the botched job I had done on myself, and rushed me to a haircut. They gave me a bowl cut; I cried hysterically about how I looked like a boy. They put a pink ribbon in my hair, the way they do with some dogs, and this, along with my mother's words, calmed me down a little.

In the afternoons, Melissa and I played with the white food girl, Paris and Nikki Hilton, and Nicole Richie, all of whom got along well with my sister. We played in parks all over the valley in our uniforms, which were jumpers with undershirts. We weaseled out of the undershirts once we were released from school, our little nipples peering out as we ran in circles. Some afternoons, I sucked apple juice out of glass bottles after ballet practice and dreamed of one day standing on my toes.

We went to school with the Hiltons, though my grandmother had been a longtime friend of Conrad's widow, Franny, who Conrad had married after Zsa Zsa Gabor. Paris' father, on the other hand, was the black sheep of the family. My mother told me this when I was young, on a drive to Paris' birthday at her grandfather Barron Hilton's house in Holmby Hills. She said, "My mother is certain Paris' family will be disinherited some day." At the Buckley Christmas party, months earlier, when Paris and Nikki showed up in strapless dresses, my mother and my grandmother had been horrified. Franny and Paris were from *very different Hilton circles*, though Barron Hilton still threw parties for white-haired Paris and Nikki. My mother told me Barron was Conrad's son, though it sounded to me like he was royalty.

The Hiltons had the best birthday parties, their massive lawn dotted with bouncy houses and croquet and tea party setups. I looked up at the looming door, which felt exponentially bigger than ours, and the stacks of floors and balconies hanging above it. I said to my mother, my birthday present for Paris dangling from my hand, "They live in a *mansion*!"

My mother kneeled down, straightened my dress. She seemed grave. I was also wearing white gloves, a floppy hat. She tugged on them, fixed my hair under the hat. She said, "Sweetie, don't use that word. It makes you seem as though you are *less* than them."[9]

Melissa[10] had a kite birthday party that last year at Buckley, since we couldn't afford the tea parties we usually had. We all wore matching white sweaters with glitter-penned kites on them.

I began to dream of showing up at school, finding myself in my beginner's French class, completely naked. In my dreams I would run into the bathroom that separated my classroom from the second grade classroom searching for my clothing, embarrassed I had shown up with nothing on. What must everyone think? How had I been so distracted?

On Easter, years earlier, Melissa and I posed for a photo in matching white dresses with pastel-flowered balloon sleeves and lace-collars. We are standing in the garden of the Van Nuys house, where we lived before The Hollywood Hills House.[11] Melissa, four years

---

9 There was a time when my mother thought my father would be famous. After they got married, my father's band ClearRock started dueling with this little known band called Van Halen at the Whisky on Sunset every weekend. Those were very exciting times. ClearRock was beating Van Halen in ticket sales all the time. My father was the lead singer and always wore these wide white pants. My mother loved being the girl with the band, the Tiny Dancer in the crowd. She had read books about Janis Joplin and Jim Morrison by then, and felt caught up in the tail winds of the '60s. Then my father up and decided he wanted to move to Hawaii *just like that.* She knew before they ever got on the plane that the band was ruining their chances of eclipsing Van Halen. The band reformed and became MoFoYa. Yes, that was really their name.

10 My sister was born in Kona, where she ate strawberries from my parents' garden nonstop.

11 Bernie's cancer brought my father and mother back to Los Angeles in 1983. She was sick with intestinal cancer. My mother stayed with Bernie, her husband, and her two beautiful sons, nursing her. Ultimately, Bernie started coughing up blood and couldn't stop. She died with her head in the toilet, throwing up her own insides, my mother by her side. It was the hardest thing my mother ever had to endure. Bernie was her only *real* friend, in her

older and on the verge of adolescence, makes a seductive face. I am warped up, gnarled hands, my chin buried in my chest and folding into multiples. I too was trying to look alluring. I have looked so long at that photo, wondering when I[12] began to imitate my mother.

• • •

Eventually, the success of my parents' business did them in. They began hemorrhaging money on vacations and fancy clothes and *who knows what else*. Their extravagant lifestyle is evidenced by pictures of my mother in London, France, Monte Carlo, at the Grammys. In one image, she poses on Rue de Rivoli in her big sunglasses, pigeons

---

whole life.

They bought The House on Kittridge in Van Nuys and just like that she was pregnant again. Life was beginning to feel like a fight to stay above water. She worked in a cubicle at the William Morris Agency until she was about to burst with me she was so pregnant. She got into the car one regular day after work, it was so late, and this was her first stressful job in the industry. She wanted to succeed so badly, and she just started crying.

She thought she was never going to get out of her marriage, now that they had a second child on the way, and that she would be unhappy for the rest of her life. My father was over three hundred pounds by then, and she knew she would come home to him stoned, maybe at his mixing board in the little studio he had set up in The House on Kittridge. This was around the time he donated his father's Richie Valens' "Donna" gold record to the Hard Rock Cafe so that we could get a lifetime membership. It used to get us up to the front of those long weekend lines for a table. They were broke and she was tired.

12 I was born on the day of the Live Aid concert. My mother watched it in the hospital, a rash all over her body from penicillin, which she now knew she was allergic to. She ate watermelon in the Valley heat. (And never understood why the hospital was so fucking hot.) Before she knew it I was running around with my hair in a ponytail on the top of my head. She called this stumpy ponytail the palm tree. Said she always saw it running, even when I was too short to be seen. My father loved us, no matter how he may have treated my mother. We seemed so small hugging him in his silk Member's Only jacket, sitting next to him on the piano bench banging keys. He never would have preferred to have sons, she would say. It just wasn't in his nature.

flying up and around her, one perched on her hand. In her other hand she is holding a petit point needlepoint bag, and smiling. I have looked so long at that glamorous photo, trying to imagine who she once was.[13]

I know she was once even, clear, tangible. Chanel perfume, swimming pools, cold-to-warm bed sheets, soft hair. She used to paint dreams on my forehead before bed, used to write words and images above my eyebrows with her fingertips. "I'll meet you on Cloud Nine," she said every night. And before tucking me in, we would make plans, decide what we would do there. After she left my father, this all became Melissa's job, along with cooking dinner each night, as my mother got ready to go out. I stopped visiting clouds, and it became harder to sleep.

When my parents first separated, my mother took Melissa and me

---

13 When they were back in L.A., my father sold the domestic rights to Richie Valens' catalogue—which his father had published before his death—to Taylor Hackford, who was making a movie about Richie's life. This gave them a huge nest egg, more than a quarter million a year for four years. Before, they had been subsisting on my father's estate stipend and what little she could bring in and hold onto. They got together with some friends and began working on *The Bobby Darin Story*. There had always been Hollywood lore surrounding Bobby's story. Everyone who had tried to make a movie about him wound up dead, but they thought nothing of it. They had an "investor" for the film, had even found an actor who looked just like Bobby. It was their chance to break into *The Biz*.

They went to Europe around that time, and it became clear to them just before they left the country that this "investor" was trying to extort money from them. When they got back to Los Angeles, they did a voodoo curse on him. They weren't into voodoo or anything. They were just very angry. Days later, they got a call from one of the other guys that was working on the film. He said that their "investor" had been shot. Some sort of drive-by outside of his studio in Culver City. They never made the film, too afraid that the extortionist would haunt the whole project.

They bought a studio on Sunset that year, which was her idea. She knew they had to fake it to make it. They moved to the Hollywood Hills in 1988 and got in with the Buckley school crowd and things were okay for a while. Or at least they had enough money to let themselves think so.

to stay in a ranch home in Burbank. The home belonged to Lorenzo Lamas and his then wife Kathleen, an actress and model who my mother was managing at the time. Kathleen had a horse stabled down the street, and when my mother was away she let me brush his brittle mane, stroke his silky back. It was not lost on me that she was teaching me to care for something.

My mother told me a few days into our stay that she was divorcing my father. We were sitting at the kitchen table. I went to the refrigerator and shaped the magnetic letters that were scattered on the side into *I-M-S-A-D*. We held each other, my sister watching us.

Finally I said, "Does this mean we can get a cat?" My father never liked cats.

"Yes," my mother said. "Yes, sweetie let's get a cat."

And so we moved out of The Hollywood Hills.[14] I helped my mother take the tiny European-style brick houses off the mantel, wrapping each one in layers of newspaper and arranging them in her Louis Vuitton bags. We glued the homes that had been cracked and broken back together, my mother refusing to give up on them. She would continue to display them on a windowsill in every place we lived.

She ordered men to lug our boxes into a brown condo near the studios in Burbank. A town whose claim to fame is the WB tower and Jay Leno's antique cars, which are always speeding through the streets. My father moved into an apartment with a black-bottom pool and a retro elevator, tucked above Sunset Plaza. When everything

---

14 She would say she tried, and only tried for so long because of us girls. Twenty years after they married, after my father had charged up all the credit cards and stopped paying the mortgage, after bill collectors had called and all of this surfaced, while my father was standing in the bathroom in The Hollywood Hills House, my mother finally decided to leave. He was in front of the long mirror in the bathroom doing something, styling his hair maybe. Brushing his teeth. She put her hand on his shoulder and she looked at him in the mirror, and she said, "Bill." She must have been crying. She said, "Bill. You know I don't love you, right?" He patted her on the back, and he said, "That's okay, honey. I love you enough for the both of us."

was packed up, my mother found that all of the Christmas ornaments we had acquired over the years had disappeared. She told me that they must have been stolen right under our noses, as we moved. She was crestfallen, and looked as though she was willing herself to cry.

THE BROWN CONDO

When my mother first left my father, she was beautiful and exciting. We rented a new condo in Burbank by the studios, and on the weekends we lay by the pool with her comedian friends, who told jokes and smoked cigarettes and flirted with her. She mixed strawberry margaritas inside and brought them out in a big cobalt blue hand-blown glass jug, poured pink plastic ice into matching glasses. My mother's chest was red and bumpy, always sprouting new freckles, growing more leathery with each passing day.

"You have to wear sunscreen," I'd say.

"I *am* wearing sunscreen, sweetie."

"You have to wear *more* then!" I'd say. "Your chest is always burnt. I'm wearing mine."

I tried to get the comedian guys to flirt with me the way they did with my mother, though I didn't understand what flirting was exactly. One of them was just starting to make it big on *In Living Color*. She was managing these guys then, and a few other actresses.

On the weekends, we played "Mack the Knife" over and over again on our portable tape deck, and spent the whole day at the pool, my mother on her stomach on a lounge chair. She resented the fact that we had to share the pool with other residents of the condo community, but we made the best of it. Her breasts sweated into her black push-up bikini. Her sunglasses fell down her nose as she squinted at new scripts, the brass fasteners glinting in the sun as she marked up each thick mysterious stack of writing and waved her hands around explaining to the guys why they were good or bad for each gig. She took breaks to watch me dive and flip. This calling attention to my body was a kind of flirting. I hit my head on the cement edge of the pool once, and she came to me when I surfaced. Her breath was margarita sweet and her hands and head were shaking. I wanted to cry but instead I studied the worried faces of the guys around the pool.

At night we all barbequed on our patio. My mother often burnt the meat, the unhusked corn. She shrugged and said, "It's Cajun!" And Melissa and I repeated, "It's Cajun!"

I went to public school after the divorce and heard my mother say *public school* pejoratively so many times. She was sad for my sister and me, felt she had failed us.[15] On my first day of public school, she

---

15 It can't all be blamed on my father. She discovered much later in therapy that it really started with her family, with the years before she ran away. Though of course she knew this all along. Really it started when her father lost his job and they left The Big Brick French Normandy in Hancock Park, and moved into that cramped duplex on Irving Drive.

In 1948, before my mother was born and right around the time the Supreme Court made it illegal to discriminate in real estate transactions, Nat King Cole put an offer in on a house in Hancock Park. Up to that point you could refuse a black family's offer if they wanted to buy your home, and people did this often in Hancock Park, which was a very exclusive neighborhood developed in the '20s by the Hancock family (who grew up in a home right near the La Brea Tar Pits). Hancock Park was made up of wealthy studio folk and other families that founded other historic areas of Los Angeles. The neighborhood was up in arms when they heard about Nat's offer. "*Oh my, he really thinks he's going to move in. What's next, the Mexicans? That sort of thing.*" Nat got the house despite the fight, and someone left a burning cross on his beautifully trimmed lawn soon after he moved in.

My grandmother told my mother this story in the mid-'60s, when they moved to The Big Brick French Normandy. At the time, my grandmother agreed with the racists, even though my mother's family had all of Nat's hi-fis. She felt they had to protect the community. My mother, who was only ten when her family left The Sunset Plaza House for Hancock Park, hadn't yet read the books about MLK or Malcolm that she read later, and she didn't think to question her parents' beliefs. None of them had any idea then that life could fall apart so fast, that the houses really meant nothing. In a few short years my grandfather would be working four jobs, and my grandmother wouldn't be able to leave The Apartment or make a simple phone call.

wedged me between two blonde girls during the morning line-up for class. I didn't understand why we had to line up on an asphalt chalk line, it didn't seem civilized.

"These girls look nice," she said. "Don't talk too much about your old school. Believe me, that's trouble."

I felt dirty in the pitiful sandbox and on the tar play yard, which had deep potholes. There was no air conditioning at this new school, no nice uniforms, and I didn't get to learn French anymore. I had to bring my lunch to school or else it was a fight in the morning when I asked my mother for the two bucks to get sloppy joes or nachos made with liquid cheese. I was embarrassed sitting at the table where the bagged lunch kids sat. We were the first ones to sit down, the kids with boring sandwiches. Usually I brought leftovers, cold spaghetti, which seemed even worse. I told the kids at school that the cafeteria pizza tasted like fried pee anyway. I fixated on this simile, repeated it often, because the joke deflected the awful feeling that we no longer had money to waste on bad, daily pizza.[16] No more white

---

16 My mother would say that my father's spending habits broke us, but what happened to her family was very different. Before the '60s, TV producers owned their shows. They were independents. Then TV changed. The studios took ownership of the shows, and my grandfather never sold a show again. The denouement came with his "go-picture" with Bob Mitchum. (They called it a "go-picture" when they were set to go through with it.) During the final meeting with the pre-production team, some young hotshot executive chimed in and asked how many Bob Mitchum pictures Universal had at the time. The answer was nine. They dropped his film.

They could no longer afford The Big Brick French Normandy in Hancock Park. My grandfather's asthma worsened. He got sick in The First Small House, before The Apartment on Irving. He had to stay in a covered porch, where the air was cleaner. My mother picked up the phone one night, overheard her father say that they couldn't afford this house either. At the other end of the line her brother was speaking, saying that he had landed a job in Chicago and would be happy to let his father take over the rent on his bachelor pad. She listened to her father, sealed into the covered porch, cough and cough through the call. My mother would say the moment was devastating: the thought of living in such a pathetic space, her own father closed into a stale room, watching his life fall apart, just trying to breathe.

food girls, no more Hilton parties.

I liked the blonde girls I had been stuck in line with, but I soon found out that they lived in small apartments and crappy-looking duplexes. Their parents were not well-dressed and they yelled at them a lot. One of their mothers spoke Spanish only. On play dates, we never went to ballet class or drank glass bottles of apple juice. We had Ramen noodles and TV trays and we watched soaps or *Telemundo* with the girls' mothers. When my mother came to pick me up I clung to her.

I watched my mother pile her hair high on her head as I clomped around in her golden glitter shoes, shoes I would never forget. She spent nights at the Laugh Factory in West Hollywood. Years later, I learned why she was so skinny then. And when I did learn, the image I had of her was punctured like black paper, light leaking in.

I said, "Mom, your hair's messy." She winked, and assured me it was intentional. I cried when she left that night, feeling stupid and young.

When she was out, and Melissa had friends over, I sat alone at my mother's big glass desk in the dining room. I pretended to be my mother, saying her last name, which would sadly never be mine, the way she did. "Loveton," she said each syllable slowly, proudly. "L-O-V-E-T-O-N. Like a ton of love."[17] Sometimes, I ignored the headshots

---

17 Lovetons never gave up easily, and my grandfather was no exception. He tried his best to maintain some semblance of the lifestyle the family was used to. He worked at the Ralphs on Western. And as a sales representative for a carpet company that catered to airplane and boating industries. Extrusions and such. He sold life insurance too. And then, because that wasn't enough to maintain the lifestyle my grandmother was used to, he and my grandmother counted commercials. My mother listened each night to the scratch of pencils as her parents tallied the ads that came on at night. Everything else was so quiet, if they weren't arguing. This was the only way my grandmother contributed to the family income, until a few years later, when things got so bad that she finally tapped into her estate money.

He came home from the grocery store embarrassed about running into old studio buddies, people that used to work under him. Now he was

all around me, put on her fancy telephone headset and played my favorite game: 1-800-DENTIST. I helped people with achey teeth find the best dentist in their area, just like the ladies in the commercials.

One night, I found Playboys under my mother's bed. When I asked her about them, she told me that she bought them for the articles, *really good articles*. She seemed to find this funny. I decided never to tell her how many vibrators I found and experimented with in her room. I wouldn't tell her how I humped the pages of naked ladies, unsure of myself. I didn't want her to think of me as sexual.

• • •

In The Brown Condo, the Bic hung from the shower organizer like the holy grail. I still bathed with my mother then, still felt awed by the beauty of her body and the way she molded it. I sat in the bathtub with my mother and she explained to me that I didn't want to start shaving my legs so young, even though I thought I did, and even though other girls already were.

"Once you start you'll be doing it for the rest of your life," she said. "Every day. Every single day and when you don't you'll feel prickly and manly. Why start a life-long chore before you have to. That's what I say." I decided I would shave my legs when she wasn't around.

I ducked under the water and pretended to be a fish and she giggled. We were naked and I was getting too old for it. We played

---

packing up their food, watching bloody meat packages turn grey in the stuffy Hollywood air. He was humiliated, and soon spent more time at the bar than at home.

Once, he had been a major player in both radio and television. In New York, he had directed *Hit Parade* with Sinatra, *The Ed Morrow Show, The Shadow, The Court of Missing Heirs*. My grandparents had been members of the 21 Club, and Sinatra often sat at their table. Mr. and Mrs. North, a show about a married set of detectives that my grandfather produced in L.A. before my mother was born, was one of the very first television shows. It was sponsored by Revlon. It starred Barbara Britton and Richard Denning. Which is to say that he was at one time a very big deal in Hollywood, and then, just like that, he wasn't.

a game she called Drop the Soap. "Where's the soap, baby?" She grabbed my foot and rubbed it on her arm, her face.

"That's not the soap, mom!" She thought I was funny. We got out of the bath and dried off as fast as possible. She said the faster you get the water off the faster you get warm. I never forgot that, it was so practical, so efficient. Sometimes, she got us hot towels from the dryer. This time, she looked in the mirror and she left me.

Mirrors always seemed to take her somewhere else.

"I'm so tired of being ugly," she said. She had her fingers all over her face, poking, stretching, picking. Her forefinger went to the bridge of her nose. "You know, when I was young, my twin sister, your auntie Melissa, threw a beer can at me after I threw a record at her. Did you know that? I had a big bump on my nose for the longest time. Sometimes I think I can still see it. But of course that's impossible."

She told me all about her nose job. Her nostrils were delicate and open and upturned. Hers was nothing like my own nose, which arced down a little, felt witchy. She called mine the Loveton nose. I also had the Loveton chin, with the dimple that was supposed to mean fame. Kids at school called me butt-chin, but I knew I would be famous one day. As she moved her hands down to her breasts, I wondered why her nipples were so much more articulated than mine. Hers were also brown and hard and mine were pink and soft and blended right in with the skin on my chest. I wondered if I would ever have such big beautiful breasts. I hoped that I would never have such odd looking nipples.

"What do you think about your mom's breasts?" she said, lifting them up, pushing them together. "Wouldn't they look nice if they were bigger?"

I stuck my tongue out, disgusted. She put a skin-colored sticker on her forehead, between her eyebrows. The box said *Frownies: Hollywood's Beauty Secret*. There was hand-drawn woman with impeccable eyebrows, no fine lines. I made a note to try these the next time she went out. She saw me watching her.

"It's to keep me from getting stress wrinkles," she said. "Your grandmother wore these from the time I was a little girl just like you. I thought her body was so strange. Do you think that about your mother?"

The terror of disappearing began then, at the age of six. I had a terrible fever, and I slept in my mother's bed all day. It was the only place that comforted me as I slipped in and out of fever dreams. The air felt militaristic. I was on a base or maybe readying for war. I was made up of that angry, anticipatory air. A blanket was in the dream. A needlepoint tapestry? The blanket may have been wrapped around my sweating body. Someone or something told me, or I had been long ago informed, that I had to begin cutting off pieces of myself, beginning with my fingers. One bit at a time. The tip of a fingernail. Half a finger. A knuckle. As I did this I began to realize, slowly, that soon there would be nothing left of me. That more of my arm was missing, I was being swallowed up by my self. I knew I would be at my neck soon, and eventually I would have to start on my feet, my legs, my trunk, my torso. All that would be left of me was a head, and then that too would have to go to pieces. I would be buried by erasure, by nothingness. My body a pile of chopped up parts.[18]

When we first moved into The Condo, after bath time my mother let me sleep next to her nearly every night. We cozied under the green-flowered bedspread, watched Rachel and Ross do their non-platonic dance. Sometimes we got the giggles for a half-hour at a time, until

18 She too had a reoccurring dream as a child. It started in The Apartment on Irving. Her mouth was stuck shut and she tried to pry it open and when she finally did, when she finally opened it enough to get her fingers inside, she realized that there was this sticky substance inside, like Plaster of Paris or glue. She tried to scream for help but she couldn't speak. She pulled the stuff out and kept pulling it out. These huge thick strands, everything sticking to her hands. No matter how long she tossed and turned, no matter how long she kept pulling the stuff out, there was always more.

our stomachs hurt or we fell asleep.[19] One night we watched *The Shining* and I was so scared I couldn't sleep for hours. I have this image of running under her bed to hide, but this never happened. I hid in the crook of her arm.[20]

When she was out on the town networking, I watched TV with Melissa. Sometimes I let Melissa tuck me in. Other times I kicked and screamed about how I wanted to watch *Phenom,* a short-lived TV show about a young tennis phenomenon. I knew my mother had played tennis when she was young, because she talked about it all the time. On more than one occasion Melissa threw me into my room and locked the door from the outside, fed up with me. I no longer knew how to fall asleep without my mother next to me.

After months of Melissa making fun of me, I went back to my own bed. My mother tucked me in the way she had since I was little. She combed my wet hair slowly, trying not to get my fine hair in

---

19 After the move to The Apartment, my mother and her twin sister Melissa sat on the floor every afternoon and watched *Dark Shadows*. My grandmother sat motionless on the couch in her housecoat, her hands folded in her lap. This was the only time they spent together as a family. My grandfather was gone all time working or drinking and at night one of the twins would have to call up the Blarney Castle on Melrose and Western and ask the bartender to please send John Loveton home. My grandmother forced the twins to do all phone business: calling bill collectors, doctors, and the pharmacy to refill her prescriptions. She wasn't too busy. She sat right there and told them what to say. (My mother learned how to have a professional phone voice, and since she never went to college she found that the skill came in handy later.)

My grandmother didn't even get up when she needed pills. She would just yell, "I need a Milltown!" And my mother or her sister came running. My mother didn't know what was wrong then, but later realized my grandmother had some kind of agoraphobia. She never stole any of her mother's pills, not even as an adult, although my father would occasionally pocket some and if he offered any she trusted it was safe.

20 After what they called rows, my grandmother held my mother tightly and told her sternly, "Don't cry." It hurt to hear that. She wanted to cry into her mother's arms, into that soft stale-smelling housecoat, more than anything.

tangles, trying not to make me cry and whine. She tucked the sheets under and around me so I felt like a burrito, and then I looked at her and smiled as I broke free and flopped onto my stomach.

"Okay," she said. "Not for too long tonight. I didn't sleep at all last night and I'm very tired too." She always looked tired now, was always telling me she hadn't slept well.

She ran her nails all over my back and sang. She hardly ever sang on key but that didn't matter. She had the smoothest and sweetest *hush little baby don't say a word, momma's gonna buy you a mockingbird.* Some nights, she told me The Long Journey Story: a princess named Moo had to trek through all kinds of ridiculous mountain terrains. She went through storms, climbed castle walls, battled dragons. What she was after was never revealed.

"Up the hill the princess went, feeling so heavy, like she had a bag of stones on her back. She felt *so heavy, just so heavy.* That's when she realized she *did* have a bag of stones on her back."

Poor girl. She made me so tired. My mother often tired herself with the girl's story. As my mother detailed the next obstacle on the horizon, and spoke of how droopy the girl's body was getting, she slipped into a snore.[21] I elbowed her awake. When she saw my

---

21 It is true that in the Irving days, my grandfather was always gone—working or drinking. But in her memory it seemed he was always right there, angry and screaming, drinking cans of Pabst, which he used to make the twins open for him. They used can openers then because they didn't have pop-tops yet. My mother and Melissa wished they could travel back in time like the characters in *Dark Shadows*, go back to the days in the The Big Brick French Normandy, ride again in their red surrey. Fights usually began with my grandmother banging around in the kitchen, moving pots and pans around in the sink, clanging them together and against the tile counter. My grandfather would call out, "Are you going to let your mother slave in her own house like a *washerwoman*?" And the twins padded into the kitchen, prepared to scrub until they couldn't scrub anymore.

He came into my mother's room when she was reading *I Know Why The Caged Bird Sings*. She must have been sixteen, because this wasn't too long before she ran away. He pointed to her nightgown on the floor and said, "What is that?" She felt so riled up by the book and so sick of his shit that she said, quite plainly, "It's a nightgown." He did not think that was funny. He

eyelids closing she paused, or sang one last lullaby verse, and then leaned in to kiss me.

"I'll meet you on Cloud Nine," she said. "What do you want to do tonight?"

"I want to tea party," I said. Or, "I want to go to Disneyland." And I'd drift off to her saying *yes perfect my angel baby*, her body close to me now, her eyes now open and focused.

On Mother's Day my sister and I wrote *momther* on cheap cards. My mother was always saying that she was both mother and father to my sister and me, so we came up with this title, which she liked very much. We wrote *momther* on all of her birthday cards too because it made her cry in a happy way. Every year on Mother's Day we also watched *Mommie Dearest*. My mother told us that my grandmother made the twins call her Mommie Dearest, when they were living in The Apartment on Irving. "I had to say *yes Mommie Dearest* to everything she said," she told us. I imagined Ajax all over a small bathroom, my mother weeping as she scrubbed and scrubbed.[22]

I began calling my mother Mommie Dearest whenever she asked me to clean my room or put away laundry. "No wire hangers!" she said, and grabbed a few from my closet, pretending she was coming at me with them.

---

was always saying that she was *fresh*. She crawled away from him on all fours. His face red and twisted up, he ran around The Apartment spraying spittle, saying, "I'm gonna get you!" (She had rug marks on her knees all the time.) He stepped on her feet to slow her, but he never hit her. He didn't have to. Her older sister, before she left, experienced something very different with him and she imagined it was much worse. My grandmother often slapped my grandfather, and then he would do it back to her. They would end up in the corner of the living room just slapping each other back and forth.

22 It wasn't *that bad*. Although, on Saturday afternoons, the twins were not allowed to leave The Apartment until it was spotless. The help were long gone now, but it didn't seem like the cleaning itself really had anythingto do with it. My grandmother was always finding a way to fault the twins, always looking for a reason to punish them.

"Let's do get rid of these though," she said. "They are rather ugly, aren't they?"

Another game of Drop the Soap. A few weeks earlier, my mother had told me she had to have a cone put up in her uterus to scrape out the lining. Some sort of test for uterine cancer, she had said. She had to be picked up from the hospital by a *friend* and was in bed for a few days. I worried, but the test came back negative.

Now, we got out of the bath and she sat on the toilet, fondling the polyps high on her inner thighs absentmindedly. Most of her body I knew better than my own. My own body was something I did not understand. I couldn't control it either. During those first few years in The Brown Condo, I slipped a disk in my wrist, broke my nose, and slammed my finger in a door after one of my first big fights with my mother. I was hanging upside down from my bunk bed railing when it disengaged. I fell flat on my back, and the smooth metal guardrail fell on my nose, ripping open skin and chipping the boney bridge. My mother came into the room, but she wouldn't touch me at first. Her body wouldn't stop quivering from the sight of the blood.

In the emergency room, the doctors accidentally broke the anesthetic needle off while it was in my nose. My mother had to leave the room. I was determined to stay strong for the both of us.

I often watched her do things like this on the toilet: play with her toes, rub lotion on her feet, inspect herself between her legs.

I knew her polyps well. She told me that my grandmother said they came from being unclean. "Your grandmother is always faulting me," she said. My mother's head was wobbling like a bobblehead on a car dashboard as she said this. I didn't know who was to be believed.

Years later, my mother's shakes began to make me feel like she was an invalid to be hidden from the world, until the first time I saw Katherine Hepburn shivering nervously, the same way, in black-and-white, her face aglow with Hollywood lighting.

She moved her hands down to her feet. I knew her toes and how much she hated her bunions. They weren't so bad then. She could still wear high heels, though she huffed about the pain every evening after work.

She looked up at me watching, and took my hands. She seemed sad. "You know when I went to the doctor it was because I was pregnant, right angel baby?"

"You're pregnant?" I said.

"Not anymore, angel baby."

We didn't talk about the abortion, not until years later, when she said to me, "Republicans[23] have abortions but they call it something different. They call it a D-and-R. They say it's a test or they're cleaning out their insides."

I said, "Didn't you have one of those?" My mother nodded her head yes, and said that most of the women you meet have had an abortion. When she first told me in the bathroom, though, I had only felt an inexplicable discomfort. I had thought, even then, that we had stumbled upon something no one, especially mother and daughter, were supposed to discuss.

I learned, over the years, that lies about a woman's body are everyday things.

Back then, I also knew her heart well. I knew to worry about her heart, but that truth came slow. She had palpitations, wasn't that

---

23 In The Big Brick French Normandy, my grandmother had lots of political meetings with Los Angeles Country Club wives. My grandfather never got involved. He had different political views, but he never argued them. He had come up in Hollywood on his own, but he never would have been allowed into Los Angeles Country Club and all those secret enclaves without my grandmother's blue blood name. And she never let him forget it.

Though she had once been a staunch Republican, the ugliness the family experienced in The Apartment made my grandmother more liberal as she got older. During the L.A. riots, my mother watched the television news as she spoke on the phone with her mother. My grandmother said she felt for the blacks. They wept on the phone together, watching footage of the police brutality, the looting. "They watch *Dallas* and *Days of Our Lives* every day just like us," my grandmother said into the phone. "They see these commercials and ads for new technology every day just like us, and they're lucky to find bread for the day. They're lucky if their kids get an education."

told me about a surgical procedure where doctors sew the back of your ears permanently closer to your head. I wanted the surgery desperately, but she said it wasn't covered by insurance.

On the way to the little studio in West Hollywood where they held the final McDonald's audition, speeding down Sunset in our Volvo—which now had a big hole in the hood—I yanked out Velcro rollers and fluffed my hair around and over my ears.

When the audition was over, I was sure I had made it. A finicky man with glasses and a nice suit came out of the audition room to give us the news.

"She's wonderful, Elizabeth. Adorable. But her teeth are a bit too jagged at the end. Smile for us, sweetie?" She put her finger under my two front teeth. "See? We recommend filing. If she gets that done, we'll take her."

I hadn't known teeth filing was even a thing until then, but for years after that I would stare at my front teeth in the mirror and rub the pad of my forefinger along them. When my mother wasn't around I took a nail file to my teeth. It was like chewing foil or nails on a chalkboard. Eventually I gave up. I had been told before that I had buckteeth, but this was an entirely new thing to hate about myself.

My mother took me to Swingers on Beverly after that audition and I ordered a huge burger. She told me that all the waiters were actors. "A lot of actors have to work to pay the bills when they're getting started," she said. I didn't understand why she was taking time off work to get me a job doing something that would just require me to get another job to pay the bills. I didn't understand work.

amanda MONTEI

THE GREEN ROOM IN THE VALLEY

My father reminds me of Sizzler, of all-you-can-eat salad bars. After the divorce, this was what our relationship became. We were always staged in a diner booth. I loved eating as much watery clam chowder and oyster crackers as I could. I liked the challenge. I ate romaine piled high and drenched in ranch dressing, and I ate it last, because my mother told me that Europeans ate their salads that way. My father sometimes ordered steak meals without potato because he had started the Atkins diet, but usually he let himself lap up several platefuls of blue cheese and bacon bits, even pastas, because meals with my sister and me were cheat days. This made every meal together feel like a holiday, but there was always food filling up the space between the three of us. He ate in a messy oblivious way, talking quickly to us, offering generalizations and assumptions about the world. My sister seemed to understand him, even when they disagreed, even when the subject of my mother came up. When he talked about my mother, I could tell he still loved her. I always nodded and went along with both sides, more interested in my mountain of salad.

He had slimmed down, and soon he was taking daily walks around Balboa Lake. Years later, his girlfriend would tell my sister and me that he had starved himself thin, had gone down to only one meal a day. But at Sizzler we were proud, happy to see him fitting into booths with ease.

His plate always seemed to clear just as we loosened up and began to act like ourselves, just as the conversation began to take off. We could never talk long enough to feel as though we were all being ourselves.

I always took two ice cream cones home.

After the first bachelor pad in West Hollywood, where I banged on his piano and wrote sappy love songs, he moved in with his new girlfriend, who in the 80's sang backup for Frank Zappa and had purple hair. He would never marry her, but would live with her for decades. Speeding down Ventura Boulevard in his old Porsche 911, on our way to his new home in the Valley, he blasted Missing Persons. He bragged about his new soundstage, which he had set up in the garage.

"*Nobody* walks in L.A. sugarplums," he said. "That's for sure."

He was designing sound for movies. My mother had told me these movies were pornographic, but I assumed she was just angry with him. She was always angry with him, though they rarely spoke or saw each other in person. He told me I could help him do foley work, could put on his girlfriend's high heels and walk in his samples of sand, gravel, hardwood flooring.[25]

---

[25] When my sister and I were away with my father, my mother listened to Tori Amos and drank Merlot and just sat with herself. She didn't smoke cigarettes then, but she sat on our patio anyway, on one of our white wicker chairs, her legs splayed out in front of her. She traced the ivy, which she had planted herself, with her eyes. She felt proud watching it climb up the stucco siding, higher and higher each day. It felt so glorious to listen to music, lay back and look. To be free of feelings that she should be doing something else.

She recalled how she and her twin sister, as little girls, had snuck into a neighbor's house to play tennis. They went swimming naked afterwards, combed each other's chlorine-clean wet hair, and then took a walk. It was one of those beautiful California days when you can smell your skin turning brown. Twin A and Twin B hand in hand. It was the only time she could remember truly enjoying her sister's company, and knowing that her sister enjoyed her company too. They must have walked to Will Wright's Ice Cream Parlor on the Sunset Strip, bought peppermints and macaroons, which came in tiny wax bags then.

They were living on Sunset Plaza, their parents had ten acres just off the Strip. Their neighbors were Tony Curtis and Jean Harlowe—who went to the same finishing school my grandmother had attended. Her parents had purchased the house after moving out of the Garden of Allah, a famous housing and hotel community where all the stars lived, after they migrated to Hollywood in the '20s. It had been owned by a notorious lesbian who

Driving to The Green Room in the Valley, I thought of what my mother must have said to him when they were married, when he was over three hundred pounds. How she felt she could have done better, and the ways she must have told him this. Must have told him how she was raised and who her family was. I felt sorry for him. Did she ever kiss him tenderly in those days? Did she ever love him the way women loved men in the movies?

The Green Room, where we slept, was stale smelling and had mirrors for walls except for a few sections that were padded. Everything was green, crisscrossed patterns on the padded walls, thick marshy green carpet. Reflections of me me me bounced from mirror to mirror, each panel reflecting hundreds of pieces of my body. The only not-green item in the room was me.

When we did stay over in The Green Room in the Valley, which was rare, I smelled skunky smoke coming up from below our room, from my father's recording studio, which had overrun his girlfriend's dining room.[26]

---

threw wild parties for all the residents. F. Scott Fitzgerald lived there, Hemingway—my grandmother told my mother this when she was a teenager reading *Islands in the Stream*—the Marx brothers, Greta Garbo, Humphrey Bogart, Dorothy Parker, *all the big names at the time.*

If only! If only she could have been a fly on the wall at one of those parties. They say Joni Mitchell wrote a song about the Garden of Allah. They eventually paved over it and put up that strip mall parking lot, where my mother took me for beef bowls when we lived in The Hollywood Hills House.

26 When she was alone, she also thought about she and her twin sister doing an impersonation of my grandmother putting on her girdle. *Oomph oomph*, weaseling into it. They did this once during one of her parents' parties, in The Big Brick French Normandy. How angry her mother was. How all the glamorous partygoers had laughed. "That is *not* the kind of entertainment I meant!" my grandmother had whispered to them as she dragged them up the stairs to their rooms. When she was alone, she thought about driving around Hancock Park in the back of her parents white convertible T-bird, driving down to the Bel Air Bay Club and playing all day in the sand. Back when Hollywood felt like a small town, when you could park your car head in on Wilshire Boulevard. She thought about tennis, which she had played through high school. She gave it up when she ran away from home, and

---

thinking of the force of her arm whipping through the air, she nearly cried. And she thought of the housecoat her mother wore in The Apartment. The one she never took off. A gray satin thing, that grew more gray and less satin over the years. Was it gray? Was it satin? The memory was perhaps without color, but not without detail. Tiny rips accumulated all over, like nicks. Were there rips? My mother was never sure where the rips came from, since my grandmother did little all day.

THE BROWN CONDO

It quickly became too difficult to split our lives down the middle of the week. My sister and I started seeing our father less. We still had lunch dates, and when we returned from them, my mother would grill us about what he had said.

"He *said* that?" she would say.

Sometimes, he gave us checks for her. Other times, he did not.

My sister, my mother and I formed a unit, and though my mother was never particularly good at archiving our memories with photos, I would remember this time because we took pictures. Pictures of us in Del Mar, where we won a hundred dollars at the races and played Boggle in the hotel room. Pictures of my sister ripping my towel off in a beach locker room somewhere on the coast, my hands covering my non-breasts, both of us with mouths wide. Pictures of the three of us dressed up on the cruise we took through Mexican waters. On the first night of that trip, my mother left us in the nauseating and windowless cruise ship room, somewhere in the Pacific near Baja, so she could drink with strangers.[27]

---

27 These things don't just happen. People don't just turn *ugly*. It isn't fair to paint her as some sort of derelict mother. If I really want to understand, she would say, we have to go back to the *real* beginning. After all, it could be said that it all started long before she was even born, before her mother or father were born, before The Apartment on Irving, before my father. These things are passed down for generations, it was in her blood. It could be said that all the ugliness really started on the frontier, with those first American ancestors. Or, maybe it all started before that, with our Protestant ancestors in Europe. Maybe all this time God has been punishing us for fucking up the Church. She wouldn't put it past Him.

I learned a lot about my mother in the condo. I learned a lot about adulthood. I learned—by walking into my mother's room when the hallway smelled skunky like The Green Room—that one has to hold in a bong hit for a certain amount of time to get the optimum high, even if your face starts to turn red and you ultimately cough it all out very hard. When I was angry with her, or when I walked in and caught her holding her breath—veins popping out on her forehead neck eyes—I imitated her. I held in my breath and shook my blowfish face in hers, and then I coughed and coughed because this was what she did.

"Oh you're so judgmental, Amanda," she said when I mocked her smoking face. "When you grow up, you'll realize how mild this stuff is."

Sometimes she told my friends and me that if we ever had the desire to experiment, we should do it with her. It would be safer this way. "You think it's *so* horrible now," she said, "but one day you won't. I just want you to know that all you have to do is ask."

Melissa and I looked nothing alike, and this made us easy prey for our parents after the divorce. My sister—with her thick dark hair and her tall strong frame—reminded my mother of our father. And I—frail and short with stringy blonde hair—came to learn that I was a younger version of my mother. Our bodies were physical manifestations, even at a young age, that informed how we moved towards and away from her.

My mother began working late, and going out more often, so at night my sister cooked me spaghetti with canned sauce and we ate blocks of store-bought garlic bread because, as my mother said, those buttery inside parts made us feel warm inside.

"You're supposed to be our mother," my sister would say. "Your job is to make us dinner."

"I am your mother," she said. Or, "Does that mean I have to do everything around here? Don't you even care about *my* feelings?"

If my mother cooked the pasta, if she was home, I'd gush to her about the girls at school. I told her one night about the man that had parked next to the jungle gym, rolled down his window and lay his car seat down.

"So I like saw something glistening," I said, and knew I already lost her.

"Did you *like* see it or did you actually see it?"

"I actually saw it," I said.

"*Please* don't use that *awful* valgirl speak."

She was becoming something impenetrable. It was as if we were beginning to speak different languages. And even though I didn't understand her, I had begun to anticipate her retorts.

She eventually realized where my story had been going. The police questioned us that week and the man was put into jail weeks later for raping a friend of mine. This girl told me at school, months later, that he had hung himself with a bed sheet and she felt very guilty about that. I cried with her, both of us unsure if we were happy or sad.

We spent weekends and summers congregating with family in the boxy suburban sameness of Irvine, with my mother's twin sister. One winter, on a rare visit to my mother's far-flung older sister, we built snowmen and saw Abe Lincoln in Washington, D.C.

The best times were in the summer, when all of the Lovetons—my mother's siblings and their children—gathered in Palm Springs with my grandparents. We all stayed in the spare house my grandparents had rented in their retirement community. No matter how long it had been since we had seen the family, my mother called these gatherings Loveton Family[28] Reunions.

28 My grandmother began compiling records of our genealogy in The Apartment. There had been books printed about the Spaulding family, which we are related to through her mother. She told us that many of our ancestors had signed the Declaration of Independence. That we were related to Oliver Ellsworth, America's third Chief Justice, and Jonathan Edwards, who was at the forefront of the Great Awakening. My grandmother

My grandparents' house, which was perched on the edge of a golf course, had an Oscar the Grouch cookie jar that was refilled diligently by my grandfather. Each day the whole family sat by any number of pools, running like firewalkers across the pavement to get to them in the hundred-degree desert sun. We were treated to lunches at the clubhouse, and sometimes my mother let me come to the sports club with her, where I skipped on treadmills and juggled hand weights, watching my preteen outline harden and soften in the mirror. I was learning that my body needed work.

My grandparents slept in separate beds and were always sighing *oh John, oh Virginia,*[29] sigh after sigh, but they were tender all over. I felt cozy in their arms. At night, when we kids weren't writing skits or songs, we watched *Gone with the Wind,* which we quoted throughout the trip. *I'll never go hungry again!* When my grandparents watched

---

read that Edwards' descendants had been cited as proof of eugenics, and even though she understood the arguments against this way of thinking, she couldn't help feeling a ***special*** relationship with history. Aaron Burr, who shot Alexander Hamilton, was, after all, our direct ancestor.

29 It is true that in the ugly days in The Apartment on Irving, my grandmother had problems, though these had nothing to do with drinking. It seemed may of these problems could be traced back to ***her*** mother, my great-grandmother Jean. When my grandmother was young, Jean could often be heard weeping. My grandmother hated her father, but she never imagined herself growing up to be like Jean. Sad and pathetic and crying. Jean was delicate and easily upset, and somehow found herself married to Richard Farmer, a boisterous drinker. Richard drank too much at parties. He publicly mocked his wife and his children and got many laughs.
Divorce was still quite taboo.

At seventeen, just after her big coming out party, where she met my grandfather, my grandmother developed Bell's Palsy, a condition that makes the face freeze from stress and exhaustion. It was right around the time of the Depression, before the family took off for Europe. (They weren't affected much by the crash.) My great-grandfather forbade my grandmother from attending the University of Chicago, because he thought women were unfit for such an expensive education, and this only exacerbated the Palsy. With time, her face slowly regained movement. She was engaged to my grandfather and moved off to New York. But of course the depression never really went away, it only hid out for a while.

game shows, they muted the commercials. My grandfather said he had watched *enough commercials for one lifetime.* Then we sat patiently together in the stagnant quiet, while they stared deeply into the silent television set, advertisement light flickering on their faces.

On special nights, we drove up to the clubhouse in matching lace-collared outfits. My grandfather held my hands and let me stand on his feet, while he showed me how to dance. There was something sweetly desperate in the way he loved us grandchildren, as if we were the smallest and strangest people he had ever met.

At the end of these trips, my grandmother stood on the lawn, making a claw with her hand, moving it up and down. The Claw was our family's signature wave, though I had no idea why. My grandmother always shook and wept as we drove off. We watched her clawing the air in the rearview mirror until we turned onto the main road, out the community's gates. "We're off!" we said. Palm trees guiding us home.

When we passed by the wind farm, I imagined myself riding the blades of a turbine like a Ferris wheel. I thought about the date shakes and outlet stores we would visit on the sweltering drive home. When we got closer to home, and hit traffic, we would pee in our date shake to-go cups, giggling.

• • •

An Australian man lived with us in the condo around the time I was going into fifth grade, but when I think of Jonathan's goofy broad smile I don't remember this kind of permanence at all. I don't remember waking up to him. I remember going to the rodeo at the equestrian center, which was just behind our house. They used to have the L.A. County Fair there, and from my mother's window we watched the Ferris wheel. The rodeo was fun. We ate barbequed chicken legs. It wasn't until dusk settled and couples paired off and began dancing—men with men and women with women—that I said, "There's something fishy going on here."

"This is a *gay* rodeo," my mother said. "Nothing's *fishy*!" She bought Melissa and me cowboy hats. We danced with my mother and Jonathan all night. He twirled all three of us.

I played Monopoly with Jonathan, and felt excited when he massaged my shoulders—the way I felt excited when I massaged the shoulders of Melissa's friends, especially the skateboarder who had made his pants out of duct tape. When I won the Monopoly game, Jonathan started yelling at my mother, said I always cheated, and that was no way to let a child behave. She didn't like that at all. He flipped the board in the air and paper money rained.

We all huddled around his CB radio at night, listened to cops talk about local crimes. This was our favorite thing to do as a makeshift family.

One night Jonathan and I built a restaurant for my mother. I set up a typed out menu, put it on top of my grandmother's best silver, which my mother washed every weekend in sudsy green stuff that smelled like sulfur, even though we hardly ever used it. We ran out of milk and Jonathan said we could use Coffee Mate creamer, it would be just fine like that. The potatoes were hazelnut, or maybe Irish cream.

"Do you like the potatoes?" I kept asking my mother. "She said yes, and pulled me onto her lap, stroked my hair, but like her, I was never easily convinced."

We stayed with Jonathan once in the spare condo in Palm Springs. I grabbed an icy bottle of vodka from the freezer in a fit of dehydration, thinking it was water, and chugged. I went to my mother, wiping my tongue and spitting, and she tittered. We had been fishing for rainbow trout that day, which was Jonathan's idea. He laughed his Aussie laugh at me, thick with bravado. The two of them were playing Uno, because that's all there was to do in the desert. "Well of course it's vodka," she said. "Water *freezes*!" I went back to the freezer and stared at that label-less vodka bottle, fish packed all around it, and whispered to myself all the reasons I hated them.

We went to see a man about a dog once, late at night. "We're going to see a man about a dog," my mother said, over and over again in the car. Jonathan laughed each time and said, "That's right!"

I was excited, because we never had pets. I thought we would come home with a puppy but instead we drove deep into East L.A. and I had to wait in the car while they went into an apartment. They came out empty handed, still laughing.

While Jonathan lived with us in the condo, we acquired several other housemates. We had Dick the iguana, and J-Bunny, both of which we bought with Jonathan. He was spontaneous, and made my mother impulsive too. We bought Dick a heat rock and fed him crickets together. My mother named him Dick, because, when she had friends over, she wanted to be able to say, "Wanna pet my dick?" Or, "Every girl needs their own dick!"

We put J-bunny, who was named by and after Jonathan, in the kitchen, but he made too much noise at night and kept my mother awake, so he was soon moved into the garage, where one night, because we hadn't fed him, he began chewing on a plastic bag that was too close to his cage, and he died. I helped throw him out, because my mother was too upset, and I accidentally hit his head on the lid of the dumpster as I swung the plastic bag up and over the lip.

I kept for years a picture of my mother in a ball gown. A black and silver corseted thing with a silver floor-length skirt. Her hair hangs to her shoulder, dyed auburn. Her lips are red and full and her face still taut. Her twin sister stands beside her. I used to tell her that she looked better than her sister in the picture. My mother stands next to Jonathan, with his heavy round-featured face. He looks strong and young and holds her tiny waist proudly. Next to my mother's twin sister her husband stands out, big and round and blonde-bald. He reminds me of my father in the Hollywood Hills days, only with paler features. My mother said that her sister paid too much for the dress she's in—an ugly gold thing—that she bragged about the price all night. They are at a work-related party on a boat, and my mother beams. For a long time that picture was framed, and I took that as evidence of her happiness. She hated pictures of herself, and I too could see that in pictures her eyes were hiding something. Years later, she told me that drugs of all sorts had circled the party. I wondered if the picture was taken before or after they indulged.[30]

---

30 The drugs started when she was much younger, but she never enjoyed them until they moved to Hawaii. My parents' friend Bob came to visit a lot, sometimes staying for months at a time. Bobby had been a close friend all through junior high and high school. It was Bobby who brought my father to meet the twins, that first day on his stingray.

When they were fourteen, Bobby and my father used to steal Bobby's sister's Porsche in the middle of the night, roll it quietly down the driveway a safe distance, then start it up. They tore through Hancock Park until early morning, when they would stop about a block from Bobby's house and push it back up the driveway. Bobby's dad was a very wealthy, famous, somewhat abusive, alcoholic figure. (Not unusual for Hancock Park then. Being an alcoholic was just being a man's man.) Bobby was there when my mother had her first hit of pot, drank her first Boone's Farm apple wine, and dropped acid for the first time. Bobby hated acid, but always had weed and coke. (His brother-in-law was a direct descendent of Wilshire, and was a coke dealer.) Bobby had tons of family money and my father, who didn't work in Hawaii, lazed around with him on Oahu whenever he visited. They went to the beach, smoked pot, who knows what else. After the first year on Oahu, they traveled to Kona with Bobby and decided to buy a house together. Bobby just had to go back to the mainland, to Hancock Park, a few times a year, to keep on good terms with his family and their money.

He met a girl in Ocean Beach on one of those trips back, and came back to Hawaii talking nonstop about beautiful Jennifer. When she came to Kona, Bobby and my father explained what they had planned. The four of them would live together, and they would all be free to have sex with whichever partner they liked.

Bobby brought major supplies of coke, pills, and Pinch (his favorite alcohol) into their home. My mother did really care about Jen, and she for her, so the arrangement worked for a while. But by 1980 my mother was sick of the party life, and there was nothing to do in Hawaii except drink, get high, and have sex. MoFoYa's drummer had overdosed a few years earlier, and the band was falling apart. She tried to leave my father, but he parked himself outside of her hotel room for three days, and eventually she gave up. About a month later, after Bobby and Jen went back to California,my father and mother went to Hapuna, had a long tearful talk in a cave, and decided to get pregnant with Melissa. That was the end of that life, at least for a while.

My mother always said she prayed that Melissa and I would not make the same mistakes she did. She wanted us to have better lives, to grow up and be better mothers. "I know you think I'm silly," she said, "but one day, when you become a mother, you will understand what it's like to love something so much it scares you."

She broke up with Jonathan right before Christmas that year, but they went back and forth for a while. The whole family was going to the desert for Christmas and she knew all her siblings were going to be coupled up and married. There she was the divorcee, the single mom struggling to get by, struggling to keep her Hollywood business afloat. Her sisters and brother had long ago abandoned Hollywood for more suburban jobs.

Christmas in the desert was fine. Jonathan did some sort of musical number with us, and with our cousins. After the New Year my mother knew she had to get a job. We weren't insured and she was always saying, "What if something happens on the play yard?" Her business wasn't doing well. We knew this. She had worked for a while trying to help my father get funding for a movie he was scoring. They were getting along, and I often asked my mother if she would ever consider re-marrying my father. She scoffed at this.

The movie he was working on was called *Letter to Dad*. Paul Gleason and John Ashton were in it. My mother told me these guys had been in big shows in the '80s. The film was based on a friend of my father's who had shot himself, and focused on this friend's fear that he would turn into his father. My mother was always hinting that the guy had left his suicide note in an obscene place. I imagined it in every orifice. The film didn't bring in any money, at least not for her. She had to give up all of her clients.

Jonathan had no job. He would eat the cheese on our leather sofa—which had followed us from my mother and father's studio on Sunset—and she would flip out and say, "How can you eat the cheese when my girls are starving? That's their protein." Some days, when we were all relaxing or cuddling up to some television, he said things like, "Why don't you get your fingers out of your arses and clean the house? Shouldn't you be looking for a job, Elizabeth?"

Every morning I heard my mother ask him the same question, "Jonathan, are you going to try to get a job today?"

And he'd say in his Aussie accent, "Aw tomorra, babe."

Jonathan grabbed my ankles and swung me around the living room. My mother was furious when she caught him doing this, and he adjusted when she protested. Instead, he taught me how to fly like an airplane on his feet. I was nearly nine years old now, and I liked having his hands on me, his big warm feet on my chest. Whenever they went out, my mother glowed the next morning, and she let him throw me around however he wanted. She said he was a wonderful dancer, and that she had never had a man love her like that. When he swung me around, I imagined we were dancing.

After she decided to give up her business, she began driving all around Los Angeles, soliciting employment agencies. She finally settled with the same company that had landed her the job at William Morris years ago. She came home from a meeting with them and as we made pasta she told me the agency was very impressed with her.

"They asked me if I might want to work for Barbra Streisand," she said, putting garlic bread in the oven. "To which I said, *obviously,* hell yes!"

I was excited for her, though I wished she had been hired by Mariah Carey.

On the day of her interview, we woke up to the Northridge quake. My sister would have been buried in books if she hadn't run into my mother's room the second the earth started shaking. I thought the earthquake was exhilarating, and told everyone for years that I had surfed the top of my bunk bed, which I had. Jonathan lit candles.

My mother got a call from Streisand's personal manager shortly after the electricity came back on. When she hung up, she said, "They said *we're on the 30th floor and we can't get up there the elevators are down*!" They had rescheduled. We all relished the day off together.

A week later she came home in her white pantsuit. I thought she looked so chic. She took us out to celebrate her new job. She would work as an assistant to Barbra's manager on the 1994 Streisand tour, *The Concert*. She felt like this was her *big break*.

After my mother kicked Jonathan out,[31] a bird began perching itself on my mother's windowsill every morning. She called it ELM birdie, because this was the name of her management company. She had silver posters and business cards that said ELM, under a seductive old glam drawing of a woman with elbow-high gloves. She looked like Jessica Rabbit. The company got its name from my mother's initials, so it was also like she named the bird after herself.

When the bird accidentally flew into the window one day, we brought it inside and nursed it back to life in a shoebox.

"We'll give it some lettuce," my mother said. "We'll bring little ELM birdie back, don't you worry."

I wasn't worried, but I liked participating in something that felt important with my mother. I felt even then that this was a memory I would cherish. Something that could be right out of a nice family movie, nothing like *Mommie Dearest*. My sister thought the whole thing was a waste of time.

My mother cried for ELM birdie every day until the bird could fly

---

31 By the time she left Jonathan, she was driving the Volvo again. My father had been driving it for several years, but gave it back since she was struggling. Jonathan drove her in the Volvo to her first day of work on *The Concert*. He was going to meet with this guy he was always meeting with, someone who dealt with investments, who he was always giving his money too. He said, "Hey babe, can I have a twenty spot for expenses, for lunch for the day?" She gave him the twenty and said, "I want your stuff out by tomorrow."

She had one of those huge car phones that looked like a little suitcase and when she got home that night, it was of course gone. She knew right away that the fucker had taken her phone. She called him to say the police had been informed. (They hadn't.) He said it was an accident, as if you could take one of those big phones by accident. She picked it up from him at a hotel on the edge of Century City and swore she would never let a man suck her dry again.

again. She hunched over the shoebox and watched it writhing around.

"It's so *sad*, watching it *struggle* like this," she said, her eyes fixed on the broken wing.

• • •

Sometimes my mother called my sister Little Melissa because my mother's twin sister Melissa was her namesake. My mother's twin was Big Melissa. Just before we left the condo my mother got a phone call from Big Melissa. Big Melissa was yelling, accusing my mother of [redacted]

"What do you think he does when he's traveling all the time?" my mother said. "You really think that's business? Because that's not what he told me. Do you think I'm the first?"

My mother's head was going back and forth so quickly, I thought she might burst. Sitting on her bed, we watched her like we were watching a film, waiting for the plot to be revealed. She rolled her eyes in our direction and held the phone away, making shocked faces. But when we tried to whisper questions to her, she threw her hand up.

The twins stopped speaking for nearly ten years after this conversation.[32]

---

32 Before she ran away, my mother sat on her bed and looked around the bare room, her twin sister's bed next to her own, and thought of how her mother had described the way her sister and she were created.

They were made of an aged egg of her mother's that had split before the sperm penetrated the two halves. Her mother had always told the twins this made them rare. When she ran away, her heart ached for her sister, who

When my mother hung up the phone and explained the conversation to us, Little Melissa said, "What did you say to make him think you wanted him?" Little Melissa didn't believe my mother's side of the story either.

"Are you kidding?"

"You must have somehow been flirting or given him the idea that you were into him."

This type of debate over the truth became a trend. My sister stopped believing my mother most of the time, and I soon followed suit.

My mother cut her hair short around this time and I told her she looked like a boy, which was a bad thing. She was getting her hair cut by Sally Hershberger in Beverly Hills, the lady that gave Meg Ryan the sweetheart short 'do, when Meg Ryan still looked like a sweetheart. This was around the time our arguments escalated. Around the time when my mother hit me, the first and only time. She spanked me hard and repeatedly because I didn't want to do the dishes. I felt like Joan Crawford's daughter in the scene where she gets beat so hard, but you can tell the ass they show in the scene is a padded doll.

"You just hit me!" I screamed and screamed this at her. "Are you that kind of parent?"

My mother talked now and then about her parents, the way things were in The Apartment on Irving. The details confused me, I didn't want to know about her past anyway. I did know she wanted to be different from her parents, and that she was afraid she couldn't, that they had somehow infected her. Already I understood that the greatest leverage I had over my mother was to make her feel that she was sick, it was in her blood, and she was just putting on a show for

---

had once been part of her. They were the kind of twins that felt each other's pains, and she wondered if Big Melissa might already know somehow, wherever she was, that she was leaving. My mother knew on some level this ache would stay with her for the rest of her life, and that her sister would never forgive her for leaving her all alone.

the world. Of course I knew what it would mean if this were true.

Above my mother's bed in The Brown Condo, was a copy of a Gauguin painting titled *What! Are you Jealous?* In this picture are two nude women. The one in the foreground, my mother liked to tell me, is Pele, the goddess of fire, lightning, volcanoes. I never could find any evidence that the woman was Pele, but this painting could also be found in her twin sister's house, her mother's house, and her older sister's house. The accretion of these paintings was something unplanned, each family member had purchased their poster without knowing that every other woman in the family had, or would soon acquire, the same print. I found this to be the most wonderful, astonishing coincidence. A sign that everything she and my grandmother said about our family, and the magic in our blood, was true.[33]

• • •

After working for a year on Barbra Streisand's latest tour, my mother brought home our guardian angel, Babs herself, in the form of a huge wall-sized poster of Babs' face, which she hung in our dining room, where I had previously envisioned myself as a telephone operator. Melissa was about to begin high school, and I would soon move to the junior high. We began to form periodic alliances with each other. We fought my mother on the poster for more than a year, because who wants to have someone staring at you while you play 1-800-DENTIST? Melissa and I hated the way the bob-cut hung around Barbra's face, couldn't stand the way she pursed her lips. We thought her music was old and boring, and we transferred

33 My mother would prefer this misremembering, but the truth is, one Christmas, my grandmother bought each sister in the family matching Gauguin prints. She was always giving out matching things. She felt that if everyone in the family had a lovely image in common, a painting of women musing, which they looked at every day, they would always be bonded in a small way.

this judgment onto her face, which seemed tight and phony. She was such a diva, looking at us like that with her off-the-shoulder dress, chin perched on her folded hands.

My mother refused to get rid of *Babs*, even long after the tour was over.

"If you'd seen her in *Funny Girl* you'd understand," she said over spaghetti and garlic bread, at the big glass table, where we were now allowed to have dinner. "Do you know how hard I worked for that? I won an *Emmy* for that concert! I was the one shoving everyone offstage when they tried to get to Barbra."

I tried to make my mother laugh. "Funny girl," she would say, looking stumped. It was one thing she didn't try to own in me, always reacting as though my humor was something unusual and surprising.

After Streisand, she landed a job working as an assistant at a big talent agency and came home with long stories about her boss, a woman named Liz Dahling. My mother always pronounced Liz's last name with such affect. *Dahhhling.*

My mother told me about the way Liz Dahling screamed all morning and then gave her hugs at night, crying from stress and calling my mother *my sweet Lizzie*. She told me that Liz Dahling bit off her own fingernails and left them on her desk for my mother to clean up. She picked scabs off of her arms and left those lying around too.

Why would a woman have scabs all over her arms and why would my mother have to clean up chewed fingernails and why would my mother hug Liz Dahling back?

When the stories accumulated and Liz Dahling's screaming escalated, my mother sat on her bed crying every night, explaining how she felt so trapped. I never asked what I began to ask in many different ways only a few years later: "Why can't you fix this?"

Instead, I sat with my mother at a California Pizza Kitchen, doodling with crayons on the paper placemat made for children, which had an empty pizza you could draw your favorite toppings on. I drew fingernails and wide, oval scabs and pepperoni to make the whole thing a bit more realistic. We took the placemat home and put it on the fridge, where it hung until my mother finally quit the job and threw it out in an effort to forget.

I tried to make her laugh in other ways, too. I often jumped out at her, from behind doors, from inside closets, from underneath tables. She always grabbed her chest, took so long to recover. I tried to explain that I only wanted to make her laugh.

I kept on, and her reactions worsened.

"Why are you so *on edge*?" I said to her, after she raised her voice, telling me I was going to give her a heart attack. I had heard the term *on edge* on TV.

Her new job brought us a Halloween party, where she encouraged me to scare guests. The party brought lots of dressed up co-workers. She dressed as the Bride of Frankenstein, with a foot-high black and white wig. Before the party, she methodically filled the garage with bowls of food, placed a curtain with hand holes in front of them. Skinned grapes were eyeballs, spaghetti noodles were brains, hotdogs were fingers, and paper lanterns décor. She set out place cards for the dinner portion, and I helped her fill them in with spooky variations of the real names. She let us each have one friend over, and she showed us off, but generally disapproved of our friends and never introduced them to anyone. I showed off too, offering tours to my friend of the spread she put out.

I walked home most afternoons from school or went to a friend's house while my mother worked late in Beverly Hills or went to the gym. She was busy and fit then.

"I hate to think of you as a latchkey kid," she said. "But I think it will make you more independent in the end."

I stuffed my bra with toilet paper all through elementary school. A few times another girl came into the bathroom and did it with me, even though her breasts were already full and warm, not boy-flat like mine. Sometimes we stripped down in the bathroom stall and rubbed our crotches up against each other, licked each other's nipples. We did this at her house after school a few times too. We made an elaborate ruse for it, even though her parents weren't home. We set up her bed like a massage table and put signs on her bedroom door and pretended to call each other and make massage appointments, and then slowly stripped each other down and began kissing and rubbing every part of our bodies against each other. I felt like I was doing something very wrong. My afterschool life felt mostly private and free, but I was still afraid of being found out.

One afternoon, we strolled around the stables near the equestrian center, checked out the horses. We had been playing in the L.A. river and I was carrying a street sign I'd found. It was the size of my torso and rusted green. The sign read *Victory Blvd.* I planned to hang it in my room because I wanted this word *Victory* to represent me. I wanted to conquer.

"This one's malnourished," I said, pointing into the stable, explaining the symptoms.

"This one's thirsty," I said.

"This one has definitely been beaten," I said, to the horse with scars on its side. "Oh my god, it's been *badly* abused!" I said. "It's *trapped* in here. What a *horrible* life this poor horse must lead. We can't just leave it here to *suffer,* can we?"

The gate must have been unlocked. We wedged ourselves in around the sweating brown. She was all muscle. We trotted her out and off she went, galloping down the hay-dusted pathway, over the bridge across the L.A. river, through Griffith Park, and up into the Santa Monica mountains. We still had several hours to kill before our parents would expect us, so we went back to my friend's house, and soon found ourselves kissing and rubbing. *Victory.*

My mother was working at her desk when I got home. My clothes were mostly dry but still sandy. "Where *on earth* have you been?" she said. She helped me wash the street sign off.

I was a tomboy who wore pants too often and got made fun of for the time I wore bright pink stirrup sweatpants to school. Some weeks I had so many best friends. We rotated our clubs, depending on school politics. There was always a new group forming, each one devoted to the focused hatred of one girl. I often got to lead the charge, pick out which girl we would pick on for a while. After I had some luck with a boy at a spin the bottle party, I was singled out to be shamed. I was thrown to the blacktop that week, had my hair pulled. I didn't tell my mother.

When my mother careened into another car, and flipped over into an embankment because she had *one drink too many*, I realized that someday someone would find out my family was unclean. I feared if anyone knew what was happening with my mother, if they found out who she really was, who I really was, I might never have good days as a hate club president again.

The memory of the crumpled forest-green Miata is smashed up against the memory of my mother giving my favorite cat away. I suppose they felt equally devastating. The kitten was supposed to be mine to keep, the runt in a litter we had already sold off. I didn't like Dorian Gray, the kitten's mother, and didn't understand her name. I had waited four years since the divorce for a cat. When we got Dorian at the animal shelter I had no say in the process, not even the naming, and I felt cheated. When she got pregnant because she spent so much time outdoors, my mother promised me a kitten of my own so I would stop complaining about Dorian's dumb name.

I'm not sure that these events happened the same day or week or even year, but when I think of the day at the impound lot, learning that the car accident spared only the driver's seat, I hear my mother telling me that she gave Dorian Gray's kitten away. Maybe she told me about the kitten when I was peering into the space where she had almost lost her own life, because she knew there was no way I could be mad at her then. I cried as we left the lot, and in the rental car on the way home. My mother cried beside me, fingering the necklace she had found on the Miata's floor. We had made the necklace together, at one of those bead shops where you make jewelry with strings and glass baubles. She had put a cross in the center of the necklace, even though we only went to church on holidays, and for days she told us the cross on her chest had saved her life.

We were used to these brief forays with God. Some days, she loved God like a high school crush, the thought of his power over her nearly bringing her to tears. She had taught Sunday school when we lived in The Hollywood Hills House. This was before the divorce, at the expensive church in Beverly Hills, where all the celebrities got married. I usually missed her class because I liked listening to the sermons with the adults, hearing the way they made sense of the world.

After the accident, my mother told my sister and I we were all *on the lam*, though I always thought it was *on the lamb*, like *lamby*, the stuffed lamb my sister and I both cuddled as babies. It played *Jesus Loves You* when we wound the metal crank on its belly. We shacked up in a hotel in Santa Barbara. I wasn't sure who my mother was running from, but I knew she had hit another car, a man with his kid, and that she feared he might sue.

"We're on the lam, girls," she would say. "So we'll use different names."

We used English and Russian accents in restaurants, saying Madonna to hostesses when they asked what name we wanted to put our reservations under. My mother kept her sunglasses on inside, but pulled them down to wink at us, shrug her shoulders and say, "We're on the lam, remember?"[34]

Eventually we went back home and my mother began community service. She picked up trash at the parks every weekend for months. She was okay with this, because she had come so close to going to

---

34 She wished she could have gone up to Santa Barbara with us after the DUI, that it had all been more glamorous, but the truth is her lawyer had screwed up her court date, and that there was a warrant out for her arrest. Who had money for *Santa Barbara*? She hid out alone at the Holiday Inn in Burbank, and we stayed with our father.

jail, but we were deeply ashamed. We told no one.

At first, she liked her supervisor, even considered him a friend. He kept her sane with his bad jokes.

"A kind man," she would say. "Not funny at all but quite kind." He must have had his eyes all over her from the start. Her favorite men were usually ones like that.

She told me one evening as she drew a bath that he had pushed her up against the wall in the office, grabbed her breast, put his other hand between her thighs, and said that he wouldn't sign off on her work unless he got what he wanted. Again I had the feeling that we shouldn't be discussing what had happened.

She had kissed him and now she regretted it. "But what was I supposed to do?" she asked.

amanda MONTEI

THE GREEN ROOM IN THE VALLEY

My father delivered the news that my grandfather had died. My sister and I were waking up for school at that dead air hour when children wake, emerging from beds like small zombies, arms extended forward groping the walls, having to pee, when he opened the door. I was in sixth grade. We were still living in the condo, staying with him because my mother was up near Sacramento, staying with her brother Richard so she could take care of my grandfather in his final weeks. His lung cancer was progressing quickly. She changed his diapers and sat by his bedside, tried to make him laugh. My grandparents had moved into a home that was attached to Richard's by a side door. Richard told my mother he was too busy to nurse anyone. My mother called Little Melissa and me often. She was always describing family conflicts that I didn't understand. Quiet secret fights about money and estates and houses. Sometimes we spoke to our grandfather on the phone, but near the end he could no longer eke out any words for us. I don't remember what we said to him, how we circled around his imminent death.

Were we still in bed in the Green Room when my father told us. Were we begging for more sleep? Watching *I Love Lucy*? Playing the *guess which episode this is* game, because we had seen every single one so many times that we knew Lucy's antics as if they were our own? Maybe we looked at our faces reacting and reflecting in the mirror-walls that we woke staring into every morning.

"Your grandfather passed this morning," he said. Talked about death the way adults always do when they speak to children. Vaguely. I began crying. Not nervous child tears. Real tears of non-comprehension. Who could I speak to about this. I was so beside myself. I had to think about what I was doing with my body and my words, and I had never felt that before. I had to react appropriately.

Did we drive through Taco Bell that morning, the way we always did when my father took us to school? For chicken soft tacos? I think we must have, but I hate to think that we did.[35]

---

[35] There are certain things my mother never forgot, that she knew she would never forget even as they happened. Great Aunt Dixie fell and broke her hip, and by that point old uncle Bob was senile and losing it too. Someone had to be around for Dixie when she got out of the hospital and since my mother was up in Grass Valley taking care of my grandfather, and had already taken time off work, Richard dragged her along.

My grandmother's sister Dixie was born deaf. Their mother Jean always felt this had been a punishment from God. She felt it was her fault. A year or so after Dixie's birth, Jean found herself pregnant again, and with her husband's support she aborted the child. She was afraid she might have another disabled child. The story was Jean had had many abortions throughout her life, too many to count. No one can be sure how they were done, but my mother assumed she had done them to herself.

On Bannockburn, the estate in Illinois where my grandmother and Dixie grew up, my grandmother had a pony, which was later sold to Spencer Tracy. Bannockburn had a rose garden and a hedge-maze, too. My grandmother was a good rider and brought home ribbons. Her sister Dixie, on the other hand, made friends with Wilhelm, the chauffeur, until he was fired for drinking on the job. My grandmother overheard her father telling Jean that Wilhelm had begun drinking heavily after he was let go. "I hear he's in those speakeasies," Jean said. "But one of my girlfriends' maids heard Wilhelm drunk one night, saying that he would give his *life* for that little girl." Wilhelm had meant Dixie. They asked him to return to work for them.

Dixie and Wilhelm got into the accident weeks later. They were stuck on the train tracks in the snow, coming home from the hearing clinic, when the gate came down on the car and trapped it. The gate guard for the tracks had been sleeping, and when he heard the train whistle he realized he was late, so he had flung the lever up, and the gate came down. Wilhelm had no time to react. The gate went right through the windshield. He grabbed Dixie out of the back seat and threw her out, just before the train hit him. His body was found tangled in the cowcatcher.

When Richard and my mother got to Dixie's big house in Levittown, New York they rang and rang the doorbell and no one answered so they walked right in, or tried to. They found themselves right up against upturned chairs and bags of trash. Wall to wall disarray. Food plates and flies. It looked as though a tornado had ransacked the house. Bob and Dixie were in their bedroom watching TV, and Dixie was all bruised up, waiting to be taken to

---

the hospital. My mother remembers Dixie writing notes on paper, since she couldn't speak. Richard and my mother extended their stay to clean up and sell Bob and Dixie's house. Richard thought it would be best to move them to Northern California.

It was only after they took Dixie to the hospital and started sifting through the garbage that they found the money. Under the bed, in several suitcases, literally spilling out of them, were piles and piles of wet moldy money.

amanda MONTEI

THE BROWN CONDO

My grandmother never worked a real job, but she sustained one passion throughout: ancestry, tracing her family lineage back to the frontier. After my grandfather died, my grandmother began mailing newspaper clippings—some yellowed, some fresh—to The Brown Condo. Some of these bits were about etiquette, and these always affected my mother immediately. At the big glass dinner table, on the rare occasions when she cooked up steak or chicken, she watched the way I cut into my meat, then reprimanded me.

"I just don't want you going to a friend's house and eating like an animal," she said. I felt like her complaint was outdated, and sometimes I went at my meat the wrong way just to make her mad.[36]

Other mailings were stories about the founding fathers—many of whom we were apparently related to—and tangential friends and family members like the painter Eric Fischl, who was somehow connected to my grandmother.

"Poor thing," my mother said when we got the Fischl clipping. "She's bored and depressed."

Sometimes, we got an obituary that had the name Loveton in it, with a letter from my grandmother explaining what sort of cousin the deceased was. Once or twice removed, third fourth or fifth. I

---

36 When my grandmother was a girl living on Bannockburn, in the shadow of industrialism, just before the Depression hit, milk was delivered to the stoop of the house in tall cold metal cans, fresh from cows that grazed on neighboring properties. My grandmother used to say she grew up in the gay '20s, and would always clarify what she meant by this. *Gay as in happy!* After all, she went to Ferry Hall, which was then one of the finest finishing schools for girls in the country. Life was very different. All of this must be taken into account, my mother would say. The way my grandmother was raised, the way my mother was raised, and the things they were taught to value.

didn't understand these titles no matter how many times my mother explained them. I looked at these cutouts and saw only a string of names. And yet, when the milk commercial came on that asked who shot Alexander Hamilton, I always knew the answer, because my mother had reminded me time and time again that Aaron Burr was related to us.[37]

---

[37] When they were in Levittown, my mother and Richard visited Sands Point, my grandparents' old country club. They had a wonderful time on that trip. Richard dropped my grandfather's name, told the club manager how my grandfather used to be the only one with access to the private bungalow on the golf course. They let my mother and Richard hang out for the day. It was the last time they were able to act like brother and sister.
They had drinks at the bar, too many drinks. A long, old-fashioned wooden bar. My mother pictured my grandparents, young and in love, rubbing elbows with the New York elite at the 21 Club. They never seemed in love after the move to California, after they got wrapped up in Hollywood, and the money came and went. Anne Jeffreys and Robert Sterling were always bickering in *Topper* episodes, but they seemed so in love. My mother never understood what was different about her parents when she was young. She never understood that the couple on TV wasn't real.

After they found the money they took it to their hotel room and counted it. When they were through, Richard said, without hesitating and with such a stern look, "We shouldn't tell our sisters about this. Let's just split it between us. We will keep it between us, and no one will ever know." There were roughly three thousand moldy crumpled dollar bills. Richard made her take half. It paid our rent that month, which was a relief since child support had been coming in late, if ever. They agreed to never tell their sisters and she never told us girls, at least not until much later when she had to. It was something her siblings, even Richard, ended up using against her in the legal proceedings, when they all called her a thief.

My grandfather died soon after the Levittown visit. The day before he passed he looked up at the corner of the room and began speaking to his best friends, his old Sands Point golfing buddies. He was thrilled that his three friends were calling to him, asking them to join as their fourth, as though death was just another round of golf.

THE FLAT ON OLYMPIC

After the DUI, and after her father died, my mother began grumbling about her commute. Working on the Westside was killing her she said, and life was short. "Rush hour traffic five days a week would drive anyone crazy," she said. "No one should have to live like this. Do you want your mother to have to live like this?" And hadn't we ever noticed how much more refined it was on the Westside? My mother was committed to the idea of uprooting us, had begun hating Burbank and its *drab* form of suburbia. She found the Tonight Show town boring and too removed from L.A.

My grandmother offered to help pay rent for an apartment in Beverly Hills, so that she would have a nice place to stay when she visited Los Angeles.

Melissa was in high school, a small public school in Burbank, which had a reputation for choirs that sang and danced provocatively to songs by Pat Benatar and Michael Jackson. Choirs that wore sequins. She and I wanted to nestle into this kind of spectacular banality, fit ourselves into the quaint non-city life the way the other girls at school seemed to.[38]

We moved into an apartment on Olympic Boulevard the summer

---

38 She understood the pain of being uprooted, but she also knew the pain of rush hour traffic in L.A. When my grandparents moved the twins into The Apartment on Irving, they had to transfer to John Burroughs Junior High, a public school. It wasn't terrible, but there were no Ahmansons, no Gettys, that's for sure. Just the average *hoi polloi*, as she used to say. She didn't know much about money then but the school was tackier looking, falling apart, and she and her sister knew that much. They had no friends and became depressed quickly. One of the girls they went to school with was a *washerwoman's* daughter. The washerwoman was on disability with water on the knee.

before my seventh grade year.

I learned how to fall asleep to the sound of late-night traffic.

My father stepped in right away, because we had pitted him against her. He was making money as a sound designer then, and still getting royalty checks because he owned the international rights to Richie Valen's *La Bamba,* and to a couple of songs by Kuiokalani Lee, a Hawaiian singer. He rented us the smallest apartment he could find in Burbank, and we used this address to keep our spots in the public schools. We never lived there, and we never moved any furniture in. He just made the payments every month, and we tried to keep our secret from the school district. My sister and I began long drives in our old Volvo—which now barely ran, and still had the big hole in the hood—over Mulholland every morning and afternoon.[39]

That Christmas, my father took us to London with his girlfriend. We stayed in a tiny bed and breakfast in the city, and he took us on the tube the first night, and when we asked where we were going, he said, "Just wait."

We walked up from underground, business men and women in refined outfits spilling out onto the sidewalk around us, and when we reached the top of the stairs we looked up and saw Big Ben

---

39 Kids often think they hate their mothers—she had—but it still broke her heart when it happened to her. Of course, it was much more difficult with her mother. They moved into The Apartment around 1966, when the draft was put in place, just a few years after the Civil Rights Act. Things were heated then, and my grandmother was holed up in front of the television.

One day, after hanging out on the lawn in front of The Apartment building with one of their only friends, who happened to be black, my mother and sister asked their friend inside, which took a lot of courage because they were quite embarrassed. They were just going in when my grandmother pulled up. As soon as she got out of the car she started screaming, "What is a black kid doing in our front yard just hanging out like an equal? How dare you bring him to my house!" She was dressed nice for once, like she had come from a lunch with a friend, maybe Franny Hilton, the only one who stayed loyal after the family sunk into a blue-collar existence. Later, when she had calmed down, my grandmother said that she had only known black people to come in the back through a service entrance. She never apologized for anything in those days.

towering over us. Everything smelled like diesel.

We went to the Roman baths and to Stonehenge, and spent the holiday in a manor house in Wales, where we watched the Queen's Address with the other tourists, opened Christmas crackers, and wore paper crowns. My father told us about Boxing Day. He said, "It's like a second Christmas." I never wanted to leave.

This was the first Christmas we spent without my mother. When we came home, she apologized for how she had hurt us, for how she had taken us from our friends. There was a tree still up, red and white presents everywhere. In a stocking, which she had hung by the small electric fireplace, was a little bunny rabbit twitching its nose and trying to hop out into our arms.[40]

• • •

In the spring, we tried out the schools in Beverly Hills. My sister had apparently missed my mother while we were in London, and was willing to try out the Beverly Hills schools so we would all stop arguing. I went along.

I was afraid of the girls at El Rodeo, the junior high. They had fancy bat mitzvahs and never invited me. They got picked up in luxury cars or by housekeepers, and I had to walk home. They all had million-dollar homes in Coldwater Canyon, knew all the words to *RENT*, and spoke French to each other. I remembered nothing of French from first grade.

Melissa had sleepovers with girlfriends from Burbank, because she didn't like her snooty classmates at the high school in Beverly Hills either, even though it was the same school where they filmed

---

40 One day, some girls were picking on my mother and her sister, and they just lost it. Started saying, "Do you know who we are? You can't talk to us like that, do you know who our family is and what we come from?" That was the first time my mother thought about running away from home. She knew that everything she had said to those girls she had heard at home. She had heard her mother's voice speak the same words so many times.

90210, and we had loved that show. I remember knowing that they were drinking in her room, maybe smoking pot. Her room was across from mine, in what my mother called our *wing of the flat*. My mother told me she had let them order pay-per-view porn. She was trying to win my sister back. We told her we felt *traumatized* by the move. I imagined them all in their bras and underwear kissing and role-playing.[41]

I spent that night wrestling with sleeplessness, loneliness, cursing Melissa for playing Jewel so loud. They must have been trying to drown out their sounds. After a while, I noticed that the smooth metal pole of my bunk bed was the perfect object on which to rub myself. I imagined myself as my mother: sort of a tease. I played the racy businesswoman that night, moving from desk to bed, having conversations with my pillow, until the pillow asked if it would be okay to ravage me, upon which I shifted, hung my legs around the bedpost, and imagined I was making love for the first time. Not sex, not fucking. I made *love* to the bunk bed. It occurred to me then that I could not imagine myself waiting much longer.

Walking home through the neighborhood, down Rodeo Drive, sometimes up to meet my sister at the high school, I sang Marcy Playground at the top of my lungs. I smelled sex and candy

---

41 Her biggest fear was that we would grow as depressed as she and her sister had in The Apartment. The twins had to take a test to get into Marlboro, a very competitive blue blood high school for girls, where their older sister had gone. My grandmother thought they could take it without any coaching, so naturally they failed. They retook it, and when my mother walked into class a few days later, Mr. Fochet, her ***stupid bald English teacher***, looked at her and said, "You just failed the Marlboro test again. You're a failure." He laughed and all the kids laughed and she ran out of the room crying, went into the bathroom and wouldn't come out. There she was living with a drunk and an emotionally incapacitated woman, going to this school where everyone hated her and hated her sister, and of course they hated everyone too. Only years prior, they had been the most popular girls in school.

Things were different for us in Beverly Hills, she would say. She was trying to give us a ***better*** life.

everywhere. I looked into the windows of all the upscale shops on Rodeo in awe, and imagined how I might dress myself one day when I was rich and famous.

Folding laundry on my mother's bed with her; the smell of my mother's showers and the realization that scents reminded me of place; doing flips and tumbles on my mother's bed while she dressed for work; the bunny in his long cage on the covered porch—I thought the sound of rush hour must have bothered him. My eldest aunt, Laurie, and her children came to visit from D.C. while we lived there, and we didn't know it then, but we wouldn't see them again for a over decade. Soon she would stop speaking to my mother.

We had backyard BBQs some weekends, in the shared courtyard of the building.

Sitting at my mother's desk one weekend, I sang *I don't get angry when my mom smokes pot,* as she carried a tray of barbeque food outside.

I said, "I don't, do I?"

And she said, "You just love things that shock you."

THE HOUSE WITH CURB APPEAL

My mother finally gave up, said she couldn't bear seeing us so unhappy.[42] We moved to a smaller home in Burbank on a tree-lined street. The house had what my mother called *curb appeal*. My mother got a new job as an assistant at a visual effects company in Hollywood, only slightly closer to our new home. Still, she was excited because Kodak owned the company, and they always had parties and lots of treats in the communal kitchen. They had a frozen yogurt machine, which I always overused on the annual Take Your Daughter To Work Day. My mother taught me how to distinguish digital effects from a real staging, by watching the outlines of each shape in the film.

The House with Curb Appeal was a tiny two-bedroom with bougainvillea climbing white trellises. At night, my mother slept on the pullout couch in the living room because my sister and I didn't want to share a room.

I had missed out on a crucial semester apparently, and it was hard to reacclimate. I wasn't part of the suburban sorority anymore. I

---

42 She couldn't bear the thought of losing us, of watching us run away to our father. She never wanted us to feel the way she had when she left home. The final straw for her in The Apartment came when my grandmother demanded she and her sister come home for dinner and she came home at twilight and no one was there, not even her sister, who was off with her new boyfriend. On the stove she found a pot of beef stew and it was cold and brown, and she thought that even if it had been warm, even if there had been happy faces around, it was just stew. It looked so unwanted and she felt just like that stew in that moment: abandoned, cold, ugly. She went to her room and the first thing she thought to pack was a book, something that would help her escape the hard reality that her relationship with her parents was failing, maybe for good. She packed up *Rich Man, Poor Man* and she felt the irony of it. She packed a pair of slippers, too.

helped my mother decorate to distract myself. We bought an antique dresser that my mother painted with thick coats of pink, then thick coats of white, then had some guy go at it with a sander. She called this shabby chic, though it looked beat up to me.

I was a fourteen-year-old girl who dreamt of becoming an Olympic diver. I had decided I had found my calling after watching Mario Lopez star in a film about Greg Louganis. My mother had watched me flip and tumble for so many years, she thought I had something, and she convinced my father to shell out the money and time to get me on the Rose Bowl diving team, a way of making up for previously missed child support months. Three times a week, we went to the acquatic center in Pasadena and he watched an aggressive coach named Aleck push my legs down into splits, yell at me when I cried about the height of the platforms, and force me to do all sorts of dives I was afraid to do. I had the feeling that my father expected me to quit, so I tried harder. My body was lean but big now, still hard to control, and beginning that kind of sport so late put me behind the kids who started when they were old enough to walk. Every day before practice I worried, but the dives and stretches seemed effortless for the other small-framed girls.

I did well, though I never could get more than second-place, and of course this gave me a complex. Still, I was able to do handstands and flips and all sorts of inversions mid-air. My whole diving team got hired to work an Olsen twin movie that year. I sat on a public pool bench and cheered into the camera for the Olsen twins' team. I changed my swimsuit and cheered for the opposing team. I hung out at craft services, and my father watched me from the bleachers. I wished my mother could have been there to see how Hollywood I had become.[43] I was the favorite for Mary Kate and Ashley's stunt double, but ultimately the casting director decided my body was too lanky to match the young girls'.

---

43 She would say we were always Hollywood. It's what united us. She knew I had the spark when I was little, by the way I strutted around in her shoes.

I was so envious of the twins as they sat in the cold pool water, waiting for the director to say action. They looked so much like me, though they were a bit younger. Their bodies still had a childish cuteness. I was all legs.

When the crew set up the shot, the twins wore oversized robes and sat on benches or were whisked off to unseen trailers. Other little girls sat in the pool shivering as the camera crew set things up. I immediately disliked the girls for this reason. I swore that when I became famous, I would never use a stand-in, would never have someone to fill my place when I was forced to do things that were uncomfortable.

I got paid a good amount anyway, though this money—which I put away in a savings account that my father had set up for me—was later taken by the IRS, to pay for an audit my father couldn't cover.

In The House with Curb Appeal we had a trampoline my father bought for me so I could practice tumbling. A few years later, my mother told me she had sex on that trampoline one night with a young animator she worked with, while Melissa and I were asleep inside.

We kept the bunny my mother had bought in the kitchen. He was keeping my mother up at night. We moved him outside, put him in the yard next to the trampoline. He would like it better in the fresh air anyway, we decided, and we would have an easier time cleaning his cage.

One winter day, we were sitting at the dinner table with my mother, Melissa and Melissa's new boyfriend—who had blue hair and wide-legged pants and went to all-night parties. In the middle of the meal, Melissa's boyfriend looked up and around the room, at each of us, and then he said, "What ever happened to your bunny?"

We all dropped our forks, and my mother said, "Oh. My. God."

We ran outside, but the bunny had already frozen to death.[44]

---

44 We laughed a lot then. That year, we spent a week in New Orleans when her company sent her to a conference. We went to a haunted plantation and my jean shorts would barely close, we had eaten so many po' boys and beignets. I got a gold star from the Paul Prudhomme restaurant, for eating an enormous

I had my own television in this house, and I watched the Game Show Network nonstop, especially at night. I realized, for the first time, that like my mother I often had trouble sleeping. I spent hours upon hours watching Charles Nelson Reilly and Rip Taylor on *Match Game*. Sometimes, I stayed up late enough to watch the old ones in black and white, with young Betty White and Joan Fontaine. I thought how it must have been to live during this elegant time, when everything looked nice, even in black and white. I thought how so many of these stars were dead now, and wondered if they hung around as ghosts, and if so who they haunted. At the beginning of each new episode, I prayed I would drift off before the show ended.

---

steak most grown men couldn't finish, and she was so proud. Melissa and I came back to the hotel room after sightseeing alone and told her that we asked the taxi to drop us off at the voodoo museum, but they left us at some strange voodoo shop, so we had milkshakes and walked through the French Quarter instead. We couldn't stop laughing telling her the story. We had seen some kind of penis shaped pasta in the window of a tourist shop and thought it was the funniest thing in the world. She would say that just hearing the laughter of her daughters at the end of a long day made that trip endurable.

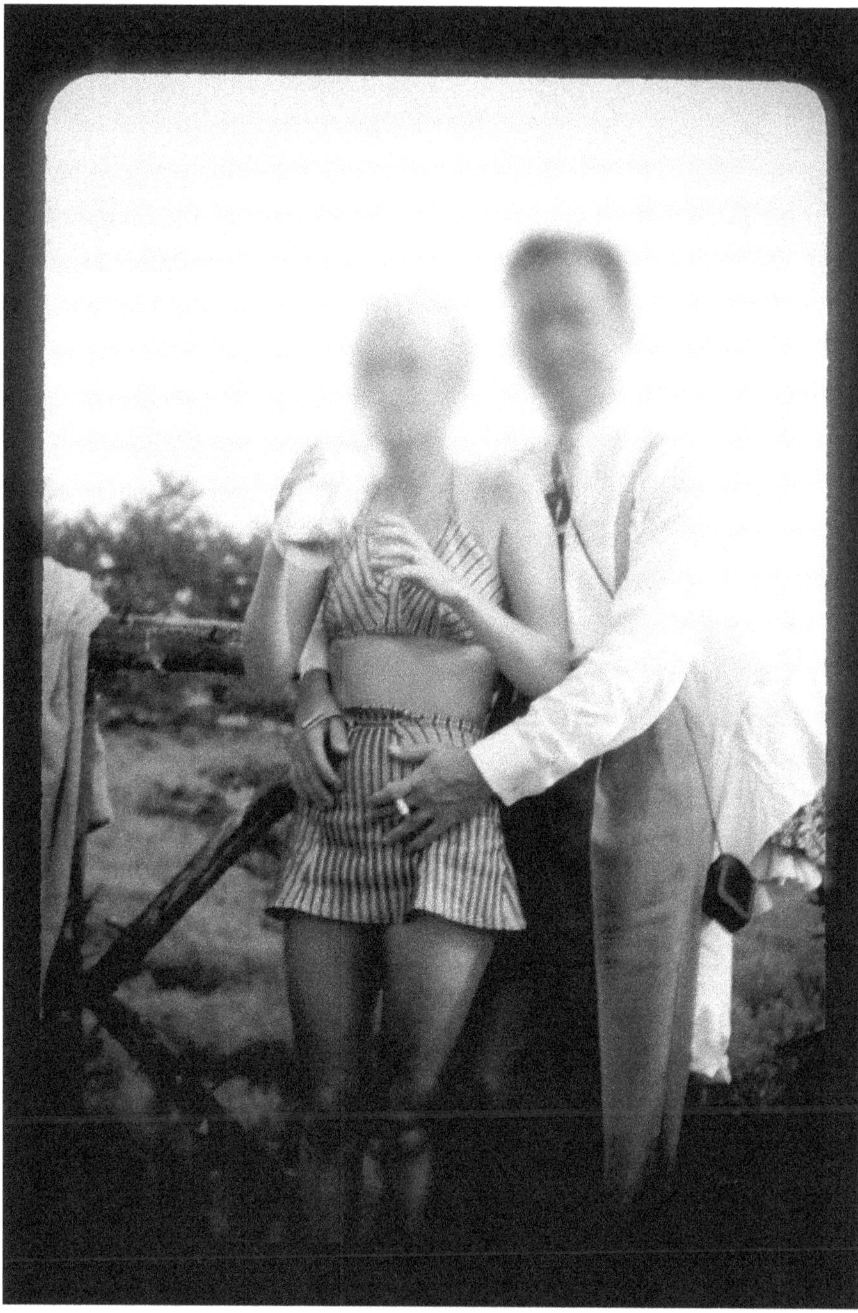

amanda MONTEI

THE ELECTRICAL FLAT

When The House with Curb Appeal became too cramped, we moved to a cheaper apartment in Burbank: a spread-out flat above a single-floor electrical company, right off the train tracks, on busy Burbank Boulevard. I began high school, just as Melissa finished up and went off to college.

Downstairs, there was a little patio that we shared with the electrical company workers when they were around, and we had an elevator that took us from our apartment down to the patio, which really belonged to the electrical company. My mother let me have friends over to sit in the downstairs backyard. We rode the elevator down, made out inside, and drank Boone's Farm and smoked cigarettes. I took shots of tequila off a girlfriend's bellybutton and then we kissed. The boys we liked watched us and cheered, Old English forties in their hands. Sometimes these boys who were older drove us to house parties with kegs and I stared out the window, tipsy, thinking these nights were unbearably exhilarating, that being drunk this way was my new favorite hobby.

My sister was back by her twenty-first birthday. She had found college in sleepy Santa Cruz a hard adjustment. She had left all her friends behind. My mother was pleased to have her back, to have young people fill the house again. She paid to have a bartender camp out in the living room to celebrate the big birthday. She invited her actor and comedian friends over. I drank slippery nipples and smoked pot for the first time that night, in Melissa's bedroom. My mother walked in as Melissa's raver friends were telling me how to inhale. I droned *go away mom* and she laughed, watched me cough.

Travis began coming around then. He delivered my mother bags of weed for a good price, and so became a regular at our house.

When I wasn't at school, I always had a friend over and we were always high. My mother kept a constant supply on hand, and was always sharing. I survived on a diet of cheddar crackers, Diet Coke, and strawberry shortcake ice cream bars. Occasionally, if it was late and we had all smoked enough, we ordered creamy pastas from Pink Dot and then fell asleep on my mother's bed stoned and full. I gained weight. I got my period.

My mother was working out of the house again, taking another shot at running her own company. My grandmother was giving her some money to support her while she got her business off the ground again. Every morning she drank cups of coffee at a new big glass desk while she read Variety and the dailies. I sat with her and helped her match clients with minor roles. We both loved finding awkward parts, small bits for extras, the *gig* it would be the worst to get a call from your manager about.

"I'm thinking of you for *Ugly Short Girl One*."

"Do you think you can pull off *Slutty Sandwich Maker*?"

"How do writers get away with this? *Disfigured Overweight Homeless Guy*."

Groceries were delivered, homework hours were lax, everything cushy. I dyed the tips of my hair pink and began to understand that to Melissa, my mother was something aberrant and weighty. I was happy that I didn't feel this way any more.

I helped my mother design lighters when her management company started losing money during the actor's strike. She bought packs of Bics and at night we'd get stoned and roll them in glue and fine glitter powder from the craft store. We found glitter on everything. In our hair. On our bread. In our teeth. We were breathing it in all the time, though it had taken us weeks to realize. We kept making them anyway, kept blowing our noses and finding glitter in the tissues.

We sold some of the lighters at our garage sales. Laid them out on an old sheet and priced them at three dollars each. When times were tough, we had garage sales in bikinis. I had girlfriends come over and we all wore leis.

Later, my mother tried to sell the lighters to some shops on Magnolia that carried pendants, candles, charm bracelets. I can only imagine how the owners looked at her, how much glitter was on her face.

amanda MONTEI

THE HOUSE WITH THE RED DOOR

In The House with the Red Door, I wrote a letter to my mother. When I gave it to her, she said I had broken her heart, felt that the letter was meant to inflict pain on her, and nothing else. She told me later that it reminded her of the letter she had written to her parents, the night she ran away from The Apartment on Irving. Like my mother, I would never be able to recall what I wrote, but I would remember that the letter came not just from a desire to name everything I thought my mother had done wrong, but to write myself into a different place and time, one where the everyday was something that had made me, not something I was living.

My mother eventually destroyed my letter, embarrassed. Burned it in the fireplace in her bedroom, where we opened cheap Christmas presents, where she laid with men and snorted coke, where I found her so many nights fast asleep next to a smoky fire I didn't know how to put out. Years later, I would feel betrayed that she couldn't allow my childish mind an archive of those days.

I'm left instead with the image of the glowing red door, the gold doorknob. It was less than a mile from The Electrical Flat, just down Burbank Boulevard, but the lawns on our streets were manicured, not overgrown or riddled with old furniture. It felt like real suburbia.

The House with the Red Door was one story, with a feathery weeping willow in the front yard. In the backyard was a water-warped deck, next to a pool, a peeling wooden bar, and a brick BBQ-fireplace combo. The BBQ was flanked by dirt patches overgrown with weeds, which we had planned to pull up immediately and replace with gardens.

My sister had gone back to Santa Cruz, this time determined to finish college and stay away. It was just the two of us now, and there we were with our very own *home* and money to decorate, the whole thing a gift from my grandmother, who was still holed up in Grass Valley. My mother's management company had caved just before we moved, and now she was out of work, had been for months. Funding my mother's only dream—owning a home—was an exultant final act in my grandmother's life. She gave her a life that would no longer be in danger of serialization. A place to make good memories, my mother said. Something to hand down to her daughters when she died. She expected to stay there for the rest of her life.

We waded through furniture catalogs and professional painters and handmade armoires for weeks before we moved in. By our first night, the whole place looked like a furniture ad.

"A place for everything and everything in its place," my mother said, as we put all of our everythings in their places. "This is *your wing* of the house," she said of the two rooms towards the front, off the living room. We decided to paint the bathroom in my *wing* blue, with a waist-high panel that had rubber ducks and said *rub-a-dub-dub!* It wasn't long before I realized how infantile my bathroom looked, and began begging to change it.

My room was plain but the den beside it got black and white prison stripes, my mother's design. She watched the painters carefully as they outlined the stripes. Only objects that were either black or white were allowed in this room.

Most of the house was this way. Each room a little world of complimentary colors. The yellow and blue kitchen. The red and white living room with a wall panel that was the exact red of the front door. The beige and brown of my mother's room matching her marbled bathroom, which had candles that smelled like sea foam, and was stocked with real and paper napkins with seashells on them. Her walk-in shower, my mother told me, had two showerheads—one low and one high—because the woman who had lived in the house before us had a husband who was a little person.

When we moved into The House with the Red Door I was sleeping with Travis, the boy that had sold us pot in The Electrical Flat. Many years later, on the day I left him, I would tell my mother that I had lost myself in him. She would say, "Humans are codependent by nature—it's not something to be ashamed of."

The night we moved in, after we had settled and unpacked enough for the day, I went back to The Electrical Flat to eat mushrooms with Travis and Crystal, the woman who had taken over the rent on the place. I ate too many mushrooms and so did Travis. An ex-boyfriend and his friends, the older boys who used take body shots off me and my few pretty friends in The Electrical Flat, were also there. They laughed from the mushrooms and their faces grew. I felt utter sadness. Travis was thin and short, pre-pubescent. These boys had facial hair. I felt younger and unsure around them.

Travis drove me home after I ate a piece of moldy bread and the streets were video games, fluorescent wonderlands. Before I got out of the car I kissed him through the window of his '69 Volkswagen bus and flew off somewhere until he pulled away and said, for the first time, "I love you."

I said, "I have to go inside now. Can we talk about this later?" I felt like I was losing my footing.

I went inside, found my mother on the deck drinking and smiling and smoking cigarettes. She said, "Oh, you're home!"

"He told me he loved me." She began to get watery-eyed and moved to hug me, looked behind me to see if Travis was with me. "And I ate mushrooms. Too many."

In my mother's seashell bathroom that night I heard the ocean. I looked into my dilated pupils, so deep and black, and thought I knew what it felt like to have multiple personalities, to hear voices, to feel consumed.

My mother took me into her bedroom and set me up with her glass bong. A glass turtle looked up at me while I smoked. She stroked my hair and took me into the backyard and said, "We own this house all the way up and all the way down. Just *think* about that." I felt like I was rolling fast off the earth, the way I used to roll down golf course hills behind my grandparents' retirement home in the desert.

Travis made his way into the house organically, first staying late night after night, then calling his mother more frequently to say that he wouldn't be home until tomorrow. Soon I told him I loved him too, and then we said this to each other too often because it felt so good at first. He slept over most nights. My mother fussed over him, paid him to do odd jobs. Hang pictures, bring in groceries when we had them, carry gardening supplies and soil in from the car. She sewed together green-checkered curtains for his bus. Travis and I sat in her room while she did this, smoked and listened to her talk about my father.

"After his little Honda car he had nearly the same bus, but I think it was a '68. Man, did we have fun in there."

She was drinking a lot but this wasn't a problem for either of us yet. She wanted to smoke with us all the time now, and was always paying Travis to run errands so she wouldn't have to leave the house. I wanted him to myself.

On Sundays, she played Joni Mitchell and sat by the pool in her bikini and by evening she would stumble back inside and beg us to take her to buy more wine while she spread butter on cracker after cracker.

We tried very hard to have fun all the time, without exception.

• • •

They say everyone remembers where they were during important historical news events and I think that's true. But I think it's true because we've been told that it is. We look for these moments. I was signing into AOL at my father's house when Princess Di passed away. We were still living with my mother in Beverly Hills at the time, and my grandfather had died months earlier. I was twelve and had been writing my first long story all day without moving, so eager for it to come together. A horror story where I described *seeping blood* in detail. I loved the word *seeping*, knew it was *visceral*. Later, I showed my mother that story and she raved about it for weeks. She mailed a copy to my aunt Laurie in D.C. My aunt recommended therapy, but my mother said she got it.

I used to spend hours in that padded mirror room at my father's house writing stories like that. He always had the best computers and technology, and there wasn't much else to do when Melissa and I visited, besides talk to him about his time travel books or the big bang theory, which I did enjoy. Talking about how huge the universe was, how time was just something made up, made my mind feel like an endless place. "Who's to say we don't all exist as different versions of ourselves *right now*?" he would say, and I'd picture another me.

I had taken a break from the story to see who was online, maybe IM for a bit, because IMs were a new, exciting thing then. I heard *you've got mail!* right as I read the headline on my homepage and I thought that it was such a *banal* way to find this big thing out. I stood up, watching myself bounce off the mirrors in the room.

On September 11, my mother woke up to the phone ringing in The House with the Red Door and my grandmother's voice like some sort of doomsday movie line. "Elizabeth, we're under attack! Turn on the news!" A lot of people got into the idea of living in a storyline like that.

She came into my room where Travis and I were tangled naked and sleeping and said, "We're under attack come look at the news!"

A tower in flames, framed heads chattering on the screen.

She kept me home from school, wouldn't let me leave the house the rest of the week. I didn't mind this much. Travis ditched school and joined my mother and me. We smoked pot all day on her bed, and she paced and shouted at the television, coming and going and smoking cigarettes on the deck, crying here and there. We had been living in The House with the Red Door for only four days.

My grandmother called back again and again as more explosions bloomed before us, as the ticker on the screen became all caps, became more aggressive. As stiff newscasters broke their usual facades, too shocked to patrol their own expressions.

"Did you hear what they just said?" my mother said into the

phone. "This might be it. I know, mother. I know it's just *terrifying.* I miss you too, mom. I wish we were there *too,* mom." And they shook and cried at opposite ends of the line.

She never really woke up after that call.

Addiction, from what I can tell, is about not wanting to be alone. Not wanting to be alone with your own strangeness, your own peculiarities. On some level I think I've always understood this.

After 9/11 we were a trifecta. Never alone with ourselves. We didn't want to be. We spent our days considering why bad things happened to people.

"At least we have each other," my mother said. It was October. We were huddled on her bed around the bong, Bush telling us about *Enduring Freedom.* We have to get them before they get us, he said, and this made sense, even though we hated Bush. If you're not with us you're against us, and so on. She kissed us both on the head. "I don't see the point in you going to school. This is right where you should be."

I said, "You don't think they'd attack L.A., do you?"

And my mother said, "Who knows. Why wouldn't they target the West Coast next?"

"But if they did," I said, "they wouldn't target *Burbank,* would they?"

"Who *knows,* sweetheart."

Was this the end? My mother took a few days off of her job hunt.

Things began happening with my mother's family, but I was so high all the time that I had very little idea what was going on and wasn't really interested. My mother was on the phone with my grandmother a lot. She left the house only to buy wine.[45]

---

45 She should have known. Richard came down just before Thanksgiving that fall. She never suspected anything. How foolish. He must have been scoping out the house, must have been plotting. He may have had the whole struggle already worked out in his head.

She would say that the Crystal story shows in some way how

Somehow I finagled from her what money I could and when I did go back to school, each morning I drank mocha lattes with Travis while we hot-boxed his van. These moments together were what were important. We had been reminded. Everyone was saying it everywhere. The caffeine kicked in and the pot wore off by third period, Advanced Statistics. I was proud to tell my mother every day that I still held the highest grade. I liked huddling over paper, imagining sample sizes and people filling out surveys, thinking how words in a question could influence someone to give a different answer.

That month, my mother bought the yellow table.

She brought it home like it was a miracle that she had found it, and she asked Travis to throw out the old wooden one. As they moved the new table in I said, "Should we really be buying tables

---

thingsbecame so tangled and misunderstood. I was furious that weekend, before Richard arrived, when she wouldn't let me go to a concert with Crystal. Crystal, the girl that rented The Electrical Flat after we moved out of it, who lived with her poor little daughter and schizophrenic father. The father who my mother was always sure Crystal had some sort of sad sexual relationship with. Crystal used to blow smoke in the little girl's face to get her to calm down, like the little girl was a dog. My mother no longer trusted her, couldn't believe she ever had, that she called her a friend and spent so much time with her. She was sure that Crystal had stolen the scrapbook of me as a baby, the one my mother made for me in The Electrical Flat. We left it behind in the move and never saw it again, so what other explanation was there?

We were standing in the backyard showing Richard the pool and Crystal came tearing through the house, screaming about how terrible my mother was, telling Richard that my mother let me do drugs and gave me pot to behave. It was an awful situation and my mother knew how it looked.

The night after this happened she was so humiliated that she stayed up late into the morning hours drinking and with sleeping pills in her. She woke up with her fingertips covered in nail polish. She was supposed to take me to school that morning but I found a ride. She knew I must have seen her awake and bombed, looking like some kind of monster with glowing red fingers hanging by her sides.

That was the last time we saw Crystal. And then, years later, there she was staring out from the newsprint. Her father had shot her late one night, then shot the little girl, then shot himself.

right now?"

"It's used," she said. "It was on sale. And your grandmother is *happy* to help."

The table was was retro, fifties diner-style, with gleaming legs figured like a woman's hips, rounding out, then in, then out again. The yellow laminate top had grooved aluminum siding, which always seemed to have a snag, some piece that was peeling away. I picked at it, restlessly, trying to just get that seam smooth.

My mother slid her hands along the top of the yellow table and said, "We had a table just like this when we lived on the Sunset strip. Of course we also had the long wooden dining table. We had a lot of tables back then, I guess."

The picture of that table, that kitchen, my mother in a bathrobe as fluffy as a clean towel, her naked legs exposed as it crept open, and my skinny fawning boyfriend, with his endless supply of pot, would follow me. At the yellow table I was my mother's baby again, curled inside her, but I was also her mother, always watching, wondering where I went wrong.

PART TWO

amanda MONTEI

THE HOUSE WITH THE RED DOOR

I am watching my mother's feet. I am watching my mother watching her mother's feet. My mother is saying that her bunions only get more ugly and more painful as the years go on. The big toe cranes up and over the second now. She is saying she wishes she could afford the surgery to fix them, saying that she forgets what it was like to wear high heels with pleasure. My mother looks up, begins watching her own mother. My mother watches the housekeeper prepare to bathe her mother.

My grandmother is tired and sick. My mother is sitting on the toilet sipping 7-Eleven white wine. I lean against the doorframe as my grandmother begins to disrobe. It seems they have forgotten I'm here. It seems to be just this mother and daughter quietly enduring, and the housekeeper liaising between them.

This bathing process takes an hour, sometimes more. My mother watches my grandmother and I think that I never want to get old. To be so close to death that I can't work my own body anymore.

I am also thinking that my grandmother could easily bathe herself, that this situation is a little ridiculous. After all, my grandmother is not in a bath. She is sitting on the tile seat in my mother's walk-in shower and the housekeeper—dressed but barefooted—is simply holding one of those removable shower heads up against my grandmother's body. The housekeeper applies soap to a loofah, but my grandmother says she will scrub herself. She will not be touched by the housekeeper in *that way*. I wonder why my grandmother can't hold the showerhead herself, wonder whether we should be spending money on this housekeeper.

My mother's face is glazed.

Once she's clean, my grandmother weasels into a robe with

heavy sighs— *huhuhuhuhuh.* Sounds of diminishing. When the robe is finally on, I think not about the way my grandmother's naked body has changed over the years, not even about how my mother's body is beginning to loosen a bit with stress and age. I don't think about my grandmother's staircase sighs or the way her laughs now end with coughing fits. I don't think about the smell of aging that has replaced the smell of the sea in this bathroom. I think only about the robe my grandmother wears, how much it looks like the many robes I've seen my mother wear over the years. I think of how my mother moves the way my grandmother does, how she depends on the same pleasures.

My grandmother labors away on the nebulizer.[46] She has to be

---

46 She would say that my grandmother was only supposed to stay for five days. Only *five days*. People should know this. They should understand the amount of stress she was under in that house. When she picked my grandmother up at the airport, she couldn't wait to see her, to hold her again, and then there she was at the loading curb with notes pinned all over, inside her coat. Medicine administration times, how to use the nebulizer and the oxygen tank, how she liked to be bathed, food she would and would not consume. Four pages, cut up and stuck all over her like she couldn't even be trusted to hold a piece of paper. My mother could hardly believe what she was witnessing. She said, "You come with instructions now, Mother?"

She would point out that Richard was already buying his kids houses all over California. Without my grandfather around anymore, and my grandmother so sick, there was a lot of tension about what would happen to all of that money. Everything was always about money for everyone. Richard said it was time for her to see what it felt like to take care of their mother, he had been doing it for so long. Maybe he thought she owed him for the house. He seemed to have forgotten the way she had changed her father's diapers every day before he died.

She was only supposed to stay for five days, and then five days later Richard called to say he wanted to take control of my grandmother's assets and put her in a rest home. My mother said, "Please just give me some time to get a job, then I'll take care of her. We can't put our mother in a rest home." And he said, "If that's the way it's going to be you will never see another penny from this family again." He took care of the paperwork and after that every red cent my grandmother wanted to spend had to be approved by him.

watched because she cheats. Her lungs are so weak now that using this machine is the most arduous task of the day. This machine is supposed to help her, she knows this, but it makes her so uncomfortable, so frustrated.

Once the bathing is over, the laborious breathing machine put away, and my mother has finished cleaning the house in preparation for the housekeeper—who will do the *real cleaning*—the day is spent. My grandmother lies down in the black-and-white prison room and sleeps, and my mother sits at the yellow table with me because Travis has arrived with a fresh sandwich bag of buds to get us high.

She has just finished rifling through the kitchen catchall drawer, looking for a lighter. She found one covered in yellow glitter. There is glitter on her hands. She found my old headshot proofs buried in the drawer, and tells Travis and I that she spent a lot of time at the photo studio where we shot them.

"You don't remember the photographer? Attractive young guy?"

"No," I say.

"We had sex on that couch," she says, and points to a vague outline behind my curls, in one of the proofs. "He shot me while I undressed, like in *Titanic*. It was the most sensual thing I ever did."

We take turns smoking in silence. I say, "Dad told me today he's going to Amsterdam this year."

"Your father has sex with prostitutes when he goes to Amsterdam," she says. "You do know that, right?"

She goes on. Says that in The Hollywood Hills House my parents owned a four-poster bed that we sold to the studios. It was later used in the movie *Maverick*. It was always tit for tat, my mother says of their marriage. "If I wanted new shoes, it was, *Okay, but only if you let me tie you to the bedpost.*"

"Don't you see why you probably shouldn't tell me these things?" I say.

Travis likes her stories, thinks she's quirky. She tells him about her old friend Dee Dee Jackson, who she knew when we went to school at Buckley. Dee Dee had died just a few years after my parents divorced, after Dee Dee and Tito divorced. The papers said that she had drowned, but my mother always insisted that Dee Dee never went near the water because she couldn't swim. She had always been convinced that Dee Dee's new boyfriend had done it, and this I thought was sensationalism on my mother's part until years later, when the boyfriend was convicted of Dee Dee's murder.

In the same way we once bathed together, now we wade around in memories, try to reframe them. It's just another kind of nakedness, and although I would never admit it, her stories make me feel closer to her, make me feel like no one has ever known their mother as intimately as I know mine.

Today I'm distracted. I'm thinking about how I've always wanted to be a candy striper. Thinking about the evenings I used to spend at the youth group at Calvary Church, playing hide and seek with soft Christian boys and wishing one of them would kiss me in my hiding spot. This was not our church. I went with one of the girls I met so many years ago on my first day in public school. Next to the church is an old folks home and one of my sister's friends worked there. I try to picture the outfit, try to picture her dressed like a candy cane and then I try to picture me in that outfit, doling out juice and sleeping pills next to that loud hip church.

My mother says something to Frances, the housekeeper, who is now in the bathroom scrubbing the shower. My mother says she is one of our oldest family friends.

"Isn't that right, Frances?" my mother calls into the bathroom.

Frances is the older sister of Teresa, the housekeeper who coddled me when I was young. Teresa went back to El Salvador after my parents divorced, when we could no longer afford a full-time housekeeper, so Frances has become our new occasional maid. My parents helped Frances get her green card. I used to play with her daughter, when Teresa was still around and my parents were still married, until the daughter got sick. Now she's in a wheelchair, after suffering a brain tumor.

Frances says, "That's right, Miss Elizabeth."

"Although I guess that title really belongs to Bob Townsend," my mother whispers to Travis. "He was my father's writer buddy even before the *Topper* days. He wrote the Avis rent-a-car slogan." She sings the jingle with Travis. *We Try Harder. Avis.*

Travis says, "Badass!"

"The Townsends used to travel with my parents," she says. "They spent time with my parents in the Keys, in Hobe Sound, in Bermuda. Mr. T used to love to float face down in pools, just like my father. They were always golden brown. Everyone was golden brown then. When I was a girl, I was golden brown—we used to rub baby oil all over ourselves and use those reflector boards, and that's just how it was then. Nobody thought anything of it. Of course we also used to cover ourselves quite a bit more—no one wore *bikinis* then, not a chance. That's just how it was then."

I cut in. Frances is out of earshot. "Can we really afford to pay Frances right now?"

"We have no shortage of wacky family stories, that's for sure," my mother says. "Have we ever told you about her father's girlfriend? Her family? Her *mother*?"

Before I can intervene she is telling us the story, long-winded. The story of the mother who took a hit out on her ex-husband and was sent to jail for—how many years was it?—for a while after her conviction. My mother is talking only to Travis now. I roll my eyes, unsure how I should engage. I don't like to hear her talk this way about my father, his girlfriend, his girlfriend's mother. Travis is laughing, coughing. "I may not get along with my ex-husband but I *never*!" my mother says. I think of food dehydrators, pasta makers, the Chop-O-Matic, the spray can of fake hair made for bald spots. Products invented by this girlfriend's brother. My mother calls them the infomercial dynasty. I wonder what our dynasty would be called.

During his infomercials, Ron describes every detail of his product, every attachment, every use, says *but wait there's more!* I want to be that sort of person some day. To be able to find an endless chain of possibility in everything.

"But wait! There's more!" she says, grabbing Travis's hand. Her eyes are slits now, his are too. I lean back in my creaky seat, fingering the cushion's loose cotton tie. "So several years she's in jail, for trying to *kill her husband,* and then, when she gets out of jail—are you ready for this? They remarry and say they've never been more in love."

Travis chokes on smoke. Frances passes through the kitchen, into my wing of the house.

"We *could* clean the house ourselves, couldn't we?" I say. The conversation deflates. I'm picking at what seems to be a surface, there's something my mother is hiding.

"*We* could, by which you mean *I* could," she says. "Besides, Frances needs the money." She tells us she has a date this weekend, drops in his first and last name as though I know the man already. She is not excited about this date and is already thinking up excuses for cancelling. It is beginning to feel like my mother has a pattern of giving up before even trying, of finding reasons why no one is ever good enough, but I feel there must be something I am missing, something I haven't yet figured out.

"How do you spell that last name?" my grandmother asks. She is in the kitchen, has walked in without our realizing. "If it ends in a vowel," she says, "don't waste your time." She fiddles with her hearing aid. It screeches feedback. Frances takes her hand, leads her back to her pullout bed. "I could go for a martini," she barks. Though she has never been much of a drinker, she says the vodka soothes her ruined lungs.[47]

My mother talks about The Apartment on Irving while we're sitting at the yellow table. I have schoolbooks piled up in front of me. Travis is packing a small calabash pipe. My grandmother is sleeping in the

47 She would say that my grandmother was very sick then. It wasn't like she was just lazy. It wasn't like it may have been earlier on in their lives. We could not afford to care for her, but no one else wanted to and my mother couldn't let her siblings throw her in a home. She began to think of my grandmother as this smelly ugly thing, an endless chore.

prison room, has just finished a long conversation with my mother.[48]

"Oh, it's just so hard," my mother says, "to hear about how angry my father was in those days in The Apartment. She said she feels terrible about the way she treated him. I've never heard her say that before."

"How did she treat him?" I say.

She holds smoke in her lungs and talks with it there. "I think she really misses him." She coughs it out. "She said she thinks he may have cheated on her, during the really bad times. But she doesn't blame him."

"But how did *he* treat *her*?" I say. I don't really want to hear the stories, they make me feel dirty. But I know she wants to tell them.

"I'll say this. Once, when your aunt Laurie talked back to him, my father said to her *you just have a hole between your legs like every other woman*."

Travis laughs. I stop, put down my pencil, ask my mother why he would say a thing like that.

She says, "Who knows."

I picture The Apartment as though it were purgatory. The walls dingy and dark, sort of leaning inward. Flames under the floorboards, bodies writhing and clamoring to get out of a door that doesn't exist.

"My mother would say *do you know who I could have married? Do you know who I come from?*" she says.

My grandfather died of throat cancer. He was not a smoker, but

48 When my grandmother was staying with us she and my mother talked a lot. That's when my grandmother told her how much she had hated her father growing up. How she would have shot him if she had a gun. That's when she found out why my grandmother always hated crying. She had watched her own mother do it for years.

My grandmother repeatedly asked, "How am I supposed to believe that my own son could be so dishonest?" It was painful to have to tell her the truth. To admit that their family was unraveling. They both knew, on some level, that my grandmother would die alone.

in his retirement he slept in the hot Palm Springs sun day after day with his mouth hanging open. Open wide, like saying *ahhh.* His gray chest hairs used to bead with sweat, the outline of his ribs poking through his thin sunned skin. When he held me close he was always warm. My family claimed that the desert sun burnt up his larynx and brought on the cancer.

"What's wrong with grandmama anyway?" I say, doodling on my homework.

My mother acts exasperated, like she has told me before. I can't keep the story straight. She says, "Emphysema. Haven't I told you that?"

The source, my mother speculates, is oven cleaner. *EASY-OFF.* Although my grandmother generally employed children and housekeepers to keep her homes clean, my mother says that in the Apartment on Irving my grandmother could be found scrubbing the inside of the oven for hours. Many nights, my mother woke up to find her sitting on the kitchen floor, waiting while the oven cleaner dug deep into the greasy recesses of pots and pans.

"How ironic to think that those nights might be what's killing her," she says. She looks as if she's willing herself to cry.

I know that everyone in the family thinks my grandmother is on her way out. What I don't understand is why *we* have to be the ones to care for her now, why Richard has become a kind of enemy.[49] The

---

49 My grandmother told my mother that Richard and his wife had stolen from her when she lived with them. Told her details of all the missing silver and heirlooms. My grandmother said there were expensive things up for grabs, that she would protect my mother's inheritance. My grandmother told her she never would have agreed to help her with The House with the Red Door if she hadn't believed that she deserved it. After all it was her money to give.

Given that it all came down to the money, maybe it all started at the end of World War I when some ancestor on my grandmother's side—who was a lumber manufacturer and sold the lumber for the interior paneling put into the original Pullman cars—was allowed to take all he could carry from Kaiser Wilhelm's castle. There was a big carved armchair, a large brass kettle or urn with turquoise inlay, her great-grandfather's own bayonet from the Civil War—which he crossed the Natchez Bluffs with. There were of course many

only bad thing I knew about my uncle was a story my mother had told me a few times about Richard's first son who had been kicked out of the house because he was *a crazy addict with his tongue hanging out.* Something about him hitchhiking his way down the coast and disappearing into the streets of San Francisco.

I don't understand why my mother still doesn't have a job, why with all of her searching, if she is really doing the searching, *nothing* has come through. There is something brave about her, the way she wants to care for everyone, the way she has taken this nursing on.[50]

For five weeks the housekeeper and my grandmother stay. We run out of money. My mother's twin sister offers to take over, and we pack my grandmother into a taxi. We stand under the willow as the cab takes her away. We do The Claw until she's off.

---

other items collected throughout her parents' lives, things passed down for generations. My mother stayed up nights wondering who would get all that history, all those objects that had been a part of her family for so long. For her, those things were her family. The money never mattered.

50 She would say she never once stopped looking for a job. That should be clear. She *gave up* her company because she didn't want to drain the estate. She worked day and night, tirelessly, to find something new from the moment we moved into that house. It was an awful climate for job hunting, on the heels of 9/11 and the actor's strike, nearing the holidays, and she called the recruiting company that had landed her the job with Barbra and they said, "Yeah *sorry* good luck *we're* all looking for jobs!" She just couldn't stand the thought of putting her own mother in a home. She was spending a lot of money on her mother's care but taking care of my grandmother was a full-time job and she couldn't do that and *look* for work, which is another full-time job in and of itself. Richard of course was already calling and screaming about the small amount of money their mother was giving us to help us get by. When my grandmother began writing checks to cover the food and the housekeeper, that's when Richard lost it. Just before Christmas, my mother decided she would go to Target to buy some gifts. When she got to the front of the line, she wrote out one of her mother's checks, which she had gotten permission to do, and the next thing she knew she was being handcuffed and questioned, *happy holidaaaays* playing in the background, all thanks to her brother.

"We had a lot of fun," my mother says, pressing palms onto the back of the red door, sealing it shut. "Don't you think we had a lot of fun?"

We have just wrapped up a turbulent Christmas, but I remember how my grandmother loved to drink with straws. How she stuck her tongue out like a lizard and wrapped it under the plastic before sucking. How my mother and I did impressions of her when we were alone and high. We also took hits off my grandmother's oxygen tank, which got us giggly. And we got my grandmother high one afternoon at the yellow table with our six-foot bong, the one we bought at the smoke shop in North Hollywood. My grandmother coughed so hard I thought we were going to lose her right there, but then she said *ooooo* and laughed her wheezy laugh.

We did have fun. At least we tried.

We are always trying to have fun.[51]

• • •

I yearn for a promise ring all through high school. Not the kind you get from a boy, but the kind good Christian girls get from their fathers. These are girls that don't drink, don't smoke. They don't care about their grades either, which seems contradictory but really nice nonetheless. They are so comfy and cozy. Their fathers all firemen or city officials or baseball coaches. Their mothers all at home, always making baked goods for school events. They have soft vanilla skin

---

51 She would say she saw a different side of my grandmother in The House with the Red Door. In a way, that was when she truly got to know her. My grandmother had given up all of her resentments. Sure, she was afraid of being alone at the end, afraid that she couldn't trust her own children anymore. All that aside, they were both more honest than they had ever been. It was as if all the walls that had been between mother and daughter came down. Later, when Richard used our time together against my mother, when he brought up the smoking incidents, my mother never could find a way to explain. She never could find a way to express how much love there had been in those five difficult weeks.

and soft shiny hair. They seem to live in a sparkly bubble.

Across the street from The House with the Red Door is the Murphy house. Their children are like this. Their girls will grow up to be schoolteachers and their boys will grow up to be cops.

My mother cries on the morning after she chased me out the door saying *maybe you should just go live with your father, it seems my presence is such an intrusion.*

She says she can't imagine how we sound, how we look, to the Murphys.

Travis tells me one night in my canopy bed that his father drinks too much and is abusive sometimes. I say, "Why didn't you tell me sooner?" We hold each other stoned and crying.

After that it's *you're just like your father you're just like your mother* all the time.

After my grandmother leaves, it seems there is always someone to be angry with. Travis for getting me too high. My mother for getting herself too drunk and drippy. She pours out these awful stories at the yellow table every night.

"That was the night I kissed Laurence," she says. She means Laurence Fishburne. She is sitting at the yellow table on a school night. Travis is sautéing canned vegetables from the temporary aid center. I stand in limbo between the stove and the table.

"Why are you on a first name basis with *every* celebrity?" I say. *Angie*, she says. Or, *Tom*.

Or she says, *Barbra*. Talks about her Emmy and drinks, gulping now because the food is almost ready and she gets excited about our dinners, as though they are private parties. She isn't really talking to me, because I've heard these stories, though she doesn't realize this. She is trying to impress Travis. I roll my eyes and kiss him while he jerks the pan around.

I feel sad for her. You have to be a certain kind of lonely to start claiming people this way, to start writing yourself into their lives.

She tells Travis that she used to talk to the bald guy from *Titanic*—

Rose's husband—on the phone, when she worked for Liz Dahling. She says she talked with Leo a lot then too, when he was booking commercials in Japan.

"Long before either of them went down with the ship," she says, smirking. I sigh. "And you know Travis, when I used to hang with Clooney at the Laugh Factory—"

Travis puts plates before us, greens beans that are nearly brown, bright corn, breasts of chicken he stole from his mother's fridge. He smiles wide, proud. She gulps and I sigh. I kiss Travis and roll my eyes some more.

She says, "Oh, it looks just wonderful honey."

And I say, "Clooney? At the Laugh Factory?" When things don't add up, I fixate.

"I think that's when we hung out, yeah. He likes comedy too you know."

After my grandmother leaves, I write a letter to a girlfriend at school. She is a cheerleader I have known since my first day in public school in second grade. Most of her cheerleader friends don't know me, because I moved away to Beverly Hills that fall years ago and so fell out of the crowd, but I have stayed somewhat close with this friend until recently, when I started skipping school. I write that I am sorry for spending so little time with her, things have been so crazy at home. My mom, I write, is worrying me and she doesn't have a job and we hardly have money to eat. I write out all my fears, tell her that I love Travis, that he loves me. I know he smokes too much and so do I *hahaha*, but he really is *good and cool and fun* and it's the only way I can handle *all this mom and family stuff.*

I fold the letter up so it has a pull-tab, write on the outside with pink markers, and pass it to her in the hallway one afternoon.

She never responds.

The bad days my mother and I share begin in the first home we are able to stretch out in. Everything shrinks for us soon after we move in, the same way my mother always says it did for her family. When they were suddenly stuffed into an apartment.

For us, the kitchen is everything. The palpitating heart of our frantic house. Everything feels small and cramped and heavy, even when we are in separate *wings* of the house, even when we are apart.

Travis and I start fighting, being around each other so much. If I am not in class, we are together, and since he goes to school with me, this is nearly all the time. One night he chases me down the street yelling how much he loves me, his head hanging out of his VW bus while I run down the street. The next morning, my mother says, "I can't believe you are turning us into *that* sort of family."

We are standing in the seashell bathroom and she plucks a hair from her chin, puts hemorrhoid cream under her eyes. She uses this cream most mornings to de-puff, but it only seems to give her orbital area a waxy, plastic look. I don't tell her this. She is standing there naked, the way she often does in the mornings. Her pubic area is bare, freshly shaven. These routines, they exasperate me. I want her to let herself age already.

She says, "Do you know what our neighbors must *think* of us?"

• • •

I start going to school more regularly. The principal's office is getting tired of my mother's sick notes. I start going again, though it doesn't feel like I'm ever really there.

We are in the line of cars one morning, and as I ready myself to hop out, she says, "To be honest, sometimes I just don't even see what the point is. I have nobody anymore."

The monthly mortgage panic has started again. Every month she is scrambling to get the money together.

"I know that's a terrible thing to say to you, and you have to know I love you so much." Her head is bobbing harder now. Her head-shakes have been worse lately. "But sometimes I just want to give up. I don't want to be anyone's burden anymore."

"We'll work it out," I say, kissing her cheek hastily. It's becoming harder for me to play a tender role. That night, we sit at the yellow table and I do the money math and it doesn't add up. She should have enough, but she doesn't. I look around the yellow kitchen, trying to trace her unnecessary expenditures.[52]

The trash begins piling up. Every Tuesday the rubbish cans are the thing. She storms into my room early in the morning and says, "Why haven't you taken out the rubbish cans?" I usually like this feud because it indicates some kind of normalcy.

"Rubbish cans?" I say. She is always calling them that. She means those big trashcans you keep outside your house and then put in the street so the trash man can come pick them up. She calls them the *rubbish cans* so we can distinguish between those and the regular trash cans—the ones we keep indoors, in the house—but I feel like it really isn't that easy to mix the two up, and it bothers me to hear her using a word that pretentious.

"Yes, rubbish cans. Do you have to make fun of everything that comes out of my mouth? A *normal* child has chores you know."

I tell her that I am not a normal child.

That's how it starts the morning I push her. She is hungover, irritable and groggy. It's a Tuesday morning and I feel my stomach burning when I realize it. I try to eat the stale cereal we got at the temporary aid center. The sweetness makes me nauseous. She is angry that I haven't taken the rubbish cans out to the street, that she has to *ask no beg* every week.

She is unloading the dishwasher, the utensils. I get up. "You can't expect our relationship to be normal whenever you decide you want it to be," I say.

52 She would say that my grandmother's five-day stay turned into five weeks, and the weeks went by slowly, but the little money my mother had saved up for the transition, into a new home and a new job, went quickly. If my grandmother hadn't offered to take care of the mortgage for the first year, she knew we would have been homeless.

"I'll just act like you do then!" she says. She throws the utensils my way and they jump up, forks biting my ankles. "I'll just make a mess of everything!"

The pain in my ankles is sharp, but I convince myself it's much worse. I replay what is happening over and over: my mother is throwing forks at me. Whose mother throws forks? This is something we can never take back. So I push her, an attempt to get her to stop, or maybe to freeze time. She falls back, tripping on the open dishwasher. She lands hard on her tailbone.

"What's *wrong* with you?" she says. I don't know.

In the car on the way to school all I can think about is her warm, sour smell, which she has from staying home, staying in bed for weeks. She is still jobless, says she is still looking, says she is so tired and defeated by the search. I go into school red-faced, my skin stained and inflamed from salt, from my hands rubbing and rubbing, trying to make my face look as though I've had a lovely morning, a good breakfast. All day at school, I think of the way my mother smells, and try to figure out ways to motivate her to take better care of herself.

Soon it's *tap tap tap* every night inside the ceiling. The squealing follows. Rats are scampering in the air vents, my mother says. She can't afford an exterminator, can hardly afford *milk* anymore. We visit the local temporary aid center weekly, stand in line for expired cans of fruit cocktail and expiring bread. Travis continues to help us get excited about these trips, fashioning meals with what we find. My mother loves when we find SPAM. This revelation makes me feel as though I'm living with a stranger.[53]

---

53 She would say that despite all the terrible things she said and thought about my father over the years, he was a good man at heart. Don't forget to give him a scene that redeems him, she would say.

In The House with the Red Door, she made me promise that I would never tell him about how her family had turned against her, about how little money we had and how hungry we were. One day, I must have given up. One

Another night at the yellow table. "I just hate myself," she says. We fought about her drinking the night before. "I'm just so all alone and you're all I have and I hate that I treat you the way that I do. You just can't understand how hard it is."

I wonder what *it* is.

She looks away reflectively, thinking of her father maybe. His angry fits, which she divulges now over and over, each time saying, "I've never told you that about my father. Have I?"

"My father just put it down one day," she says. "He just woke up one day and said *nope that's it I'm done*. Never touched another drop. He had such will."

"Sometimes it's best to stop talking about things," I say to her. Travis is making canned beef stew. "Sometimes the worst thing you can do is to keep talking about things."

She sighs deeply and goes outside, smokes cigarettes through dinner, refuses to come inside to eat. I know she has a bottle of wine in her room. Tonight, she's keeping it hidden.[54]

---

day, not long after my grandmother had left, after having lunch together, my father and I surprised my mother. She would say she never forgot the feeling of looking out the window, happy enough to have me home, and there he was in the driveway with his Porsche filled with groceries. She figured he must have bought them, rather than just given her the money, because he didn't trust her with the money. Maybe I was to blame for that. Maybe he wanted to control his giving, like he had always wanted to control everything. It didn't matter then. She hugged him so close and cried, thanked him. He whispered to her, "You know I'll always love you." He was the only person who ever came to help us.

54 After my grandmother left they spoke on the phone but it was very difficult. My grandmother knew my mother had no source of income and none in the bank and still she'd ask, "Did you get a job yet? Are things better?"

"No, mother, I don't have a job," she would say, "they're going to cut the phone off because you ran up a nine-hundred-dollar phone bill that I can't pay and I have no money for gas, food or utilities." She would concede that it was hard for my grandmother as well, because it broke her heart that her daughter was in so much pain and there was nothing she could do, except say the wrong thing and make it all worse.

Everything she does is itchy.

I make the mistake of throwing her oversized bottle of wine into the sink one night, shattering it. I throw her cigarettes into the disposal, flip the switch. She walks four blocks in my old diving team parka to the 7-Eleven for replacements. I go to school red-faced again, after we fight all night and all morning about her drinking.[55]

An hour before lunch, she comes to get me at school. This is a repeated routine. She feels guilty, and uses that as a reason to call in sick to work. Then she picks me up so we can get high and feel like we've made up. On this particular morning I have swallowed so much snot from crying that I find myself in the nurse's office complaining of a stomachache, eating little cookies, drinking Dixie cups of water, trying to fortify and breathe a little before Anatomy. I don't like to miss class if I'm in this kind of mood. Lessons keep my mind busy.[56]

I find my mother in the hallway on my way back to class. She is stomping out of the school. I missed her call to the office and the administration didn't know where I was.

"I thought you were dead!" she says. "I thought you had finally

---

55 She also made a couple of calls to the family after my grandmother left. They told her that if she ever called any of them again, including her own mother, it was just a "call for pain." They all said that, like it had been orchestrated.

She went into AA briefly in January. Her sponsor said that if the family called lovingly she could talk to them, otherwise she had to cut them all off or never recover. She did stop calling and no one ever called her. She had no contact with anyone until she tried to reach my grandmother on her birthday months later. Richard refused to give her my grandmother's number, and her sisters said they couldn't give it to her either, or Richard would write them out of their inheritance. So she gave up. She didn't even know where my grandmother was living.

56 A month or so later my grandmother called out of the blue. Her head had cleared for a moment and our number just came to her, just like that. She told my mother that the family had taken her phone book. She said she had been sitting in an old folks home in Southern California since the day she left.

run away! What were you thinking? Where were you?"

In the car, she lays the silence on thick until we park under a melancholy tree. She turns and says she has thought a lot about the morning and the night before.[57] She says she knows I don't understand her actions, what she's going through, what she's feeling, but *things are very stressful* right now, worse than they've ever been. I ask her if we can just go home. She says she knows I don't understand, but sometimes she wishes so badly I would try. As she speaks, her body is consumed by tremors.

I start hearing about her therapists after that day in the car. I hate them, they get everything wrong and always side with her. After a therapy day, everything triggers her. Everything is metaphor or an example of *the problem.*

"I think my twin sister has never forgiven me for running away and leaving her in that apartment all alone," she says one day after therapy. "But what was I supposed to do?"

Another day after therapy. "I think your sister still blames me for breaking up our family and not allowing you two to have a nuclear family. But what was I supposed to do?"

Another day after therapy, after a few glasses of wine. "My therapist says you are trying to control me. You really have to let me go."

This comes after I confront her on the deck, where she is smoking and sipping and teetering. I say, "You're falling *over.* Do you tell your

---

57 She would say that it broke her heart that her siblings didn't ever call to check on her. Didn't bring her a casserole or even a sandwich, couldn't even be bothered to speak to her, and less than a year ago they had all been a normal loving family. That summer we had a garage sale on the driveway with some of those AA people—she can't imagine how it must have looked to the neighbors, these toothless guys helping her out. She sold the whole set of her great-grandmother's beautiful pink-rimmed Limoges china plates for thirty-five dollars. Soon after she sold some white gold spoons, which my grandmother had given to her before she left. We were flat broke and she suspected the pawn shop guy was lying when he said they weren't real gold, but how could she be sure? She never did see them tarnish but had no choice but to sell anyway. She felt physically sick as she let those things go.

therapist that?"

"Oh *stop*," she says. "I'm an adult. Adults are allowed to have some time off. You're just angry because I have finally decided to start living for myself."

But it's bad day, good day time off. Always time off. Everything is either too horrible or too wonderful to stand without some Chardonnay. If my mother had friends and was doing this out—not on the back deck smoking and staring at nothing—maybe it wouldn't be so bad. I wouldn't have to see it, could still think of her as a mother.

"I think you need someone," I say. "I think you're just bored."

She doesn't like socializing, prefers the solitude of home. She's said this before. She says she hates men too. She hasn't dated anyone since we moved into the house.

"You sound like my mother," she says. "That's sweet, but a man won't get me a *job*. Besides, they're a waste of time. All men want is to screw you. I'd much prefer to be alone with a glass of wine and a book any day."

But she's stopped reading lately, stopped coming home with bags of books, stopped telling me in the mornings about what she's read the night before.

"Maybe I should be a lesbian," she says. She smiles wide, thinks it is her best joke. "Every fucking man is an *asshole*. I mean *really*."

I imagine her meeting a lovely woman who understands her in ways I can't. I imagine her feeling cherished.

My mother asks me if I might think about calling my uncle Richard, to tell him that we need support, some money.[58] He won't take her calls. I think this is because we couldn't afford to continue to care for my grandmother, but I'm unsure. I am too high, and I don't want to think about any of it anyway.

"Maybe he will listen if it comes from you," she says. We are

58 She would insist I offered to call Richard, was always by her side defending her.

breaking open microwaved baked potatoes. They're growing eyes. My mother slops on sour cream and butter, sips her Pinot Grigio.

I want her to make things orderly again.

"Maybe you should just stop buying wine," I say.[59] She leaves the table and smokes cigarettes outside for hours. Her potato stays on the table all night, a reminder of the way I spoiled the night.[60]

I call Richard the next day and find myself crying on the phone, overcome with desperation.[61] It all feels melodramatic but I can't stop myself. It occurs to me that sometimes life needs to be acted out this way.

"We've supported you long enough," he says, "We don't give a fuck about your family anymore."[62]

I hang up.[63] I tell my mother what he said and she gets hysterical.[64] I too am raging inside. I don't understand why he would say a thing like that.

My mother says, "Did you hear a glass clinking?"

I say I think I might have, because I want an answer too.[65]

---

59 She drank a lot then but even if she hadn't we were so fucked financially that there was nothing she could do. Drinking was the only way she kept from losing it.

60 She went over her options in her head night after night, trying to find a way out of the mess.

61 She almost gave up many many times, so many nights she couldn't keep from crying.

62 She never forgot the way I stood up for her.

63 The way I said to Richard, "How dare you." The way I said, "It's your niece, remember? We're your family, remember? We love you. Remember?"

64 She couldn't believe he had grown to hate his own sister so much, and for what? Because she struggled?

65 She couldn't believe what *the disease* was doing to him, but she also couldn't blame him, that was the worst of it. She couldn't blame any of her

"Fucking drunk," she says. "Just like my father."[66]

• • •

My grandmother dies in the Fall, six months after she is put into a home in Orange County just miles from Big Melissa and her family, who is still living in a subdivision in Irvine. Big Melissa claims that her family visited my grandmother often in the home. My mother has not been allowed this privilege, but when it becomes apparent that my grandmother could only have a few weeks left, she receives a call.

This final visit is an event. She asks Little Melissa to come home from college for the trip. She needs someone there for support, and I refuse to be that someone.

My mother is trying not to drink anymore, going to meetings even though she says the AA people are cultish. Too godly and hand-holdy.

"I know that going down there is going to send me into a depressed state," she says before leaving the house.

I tell her it will if she tells herself it will.

The room my grandmother is staying in is filled with framed pictures of Big Melissa's kids, Richard and his family, and the family of my mother's big sister Laurie—who has been quiet on the east coast, not wanting to take sides. There are no pictures of our family.

"It's like we've been erased," my mother tells me on the phone.[67]

---

family for their shortcomings, when she really got honest with herself.

66 Her brother and sisters had all been hurt so many years ago. They were all still hurting so much, and she felt like the only one who could admit it.

67 She would say my grandmother understood the way the family was pushing my mother out. My mother and sister sat with her during her last weekend in California, held her hand and talked of the way things had begun to fall apart. This is when my grandmother said, "Promise me you will tell our story." And my mother knew that somehow, someday, she would.

That night, as I smoke at the yellow table alone with Travis, I think of my grandmother forgetting me, dying without any idea of who I am. I imagine my mother and sister hearing my grandmother's last words without me, strained words truncated by a slip in breath, punctuated by the last closing of her eyelids. I wonder if I will ever forgive myself for refusing to go on the trip.[68]

When my mother comes home Sunday evening, she tells me she fell off the wagon hard, in the hotel lobby that night.[69] My grandmother dies weeks later and more court documents begin rolling in. Richard wants the deed to the house. My grandmother was tricked into the agreement, he says, and now The House with the Red Door has to be absorbed into the estate officially. My mother, he says, has always been manipulative. She has always been a freeloader, the abusive daughter who ran away from home, the drug addict.

Days later, I hear my mother come inside after a cigarette. It's a quiet weekend, but the door slams shut behind her. The Santa Anas have been slamming doors all day. Travis and I are smoking in my room, avoiding her, but we hear the door. Then I hear her gasp and curse.

I find my mother crying, hunched over the washing machine, which sits inside an alcove in the kitchen, next to the yellow table. She tells me in tears that during that last visit she snuck my grandmother's housecoat out of the hospice, brought it home, and has been sleeping beside it. She has washed it by mistake. I sit at the yellow table and watch her body quiver.

I pour over bits of color, scent, texture, whatever I can dig up.

---

68 She would say my grandmother's last words were weeks after that final visit, after Big Melissa chose to move her into a home in Washington, D.C. She would say that it was that move that killed her. My grandmother died alone, and her death pushed my mother over the edge, ended her brief stint with sobriety.

69 She would say she stayed sober that weekend. She wanted to remember her mother as best she could, wanted her eyes and mind to be clear. It was one of the hardest things she ever did.

Not sure if I'm trying for myself, or for her. I try to remember what it felt like to be held by my grandmother, to be pressed against that final ice-blue satin housecoat. How her flesh felt through it, how far my arms wrapped around her body. I know that her scent was once familiar to me, something I could almost call up at will.

Powder?

Why can't I cry in front of the television when the news airs, the way my mother does? Why can't I go to my mother now and hold her? Why can't I fall apart, when I think of grandmother? When my grandfather died, I had to sing "Amazing Grace" in front of my grandfather's ashes, and I lost my breath the moment I began singing.

I guess I've lost something.

I wonder whether, when we get older, we realize what we are supposed to do when big things like death happen, and the feelings that once raced through us find stopping points, little dams. There is too much pressure to mourn in this house, has been for days, and I'm not sure of the right way to do it. On TV, I have heard that we love death and fear now. We love to hear that people are dying and suffering because we get to breathe relief, knowing that we are okay. I think of all the Lovetons laying in a row, on lounge chairs in Palm Springs, on a sweltering day. *Mouths open wide saying ahhhhh.*

I watch her body give into the pain, and it seems I can hear her thoughts. *She's gone she's gone she's gone forever.* The air hanging above and around the yellow table is staticky, filled with energy, like she brought the Santa Ana winds—which are whistling now, and whipping the willow tree on the front lawn—inside. I think I should feel death the way she does, but I never ever want to.

"Memories are more important than *things,*" I say. She nods unconvincingly.

"I so wish that I had loved her more openly when she was alive," she says. She moves the housecoat into the dryer.[70]

---

70 She would say there are so many things she wishes she had probed my grandmother about. So many things she wishes she knew. The name

• • •

Spring is a slow, unsteady rebirth.

For the first year after September 11, we thought Bush had everything handled, even though my mother had plenty of negative things to say about his family. My mother said, "What other choice do we have?" But over the past year, though we have hardly been focused on much outside of the house, my mother has become suspicious and news anchors have begun to talk. Now, two years later, we watch our country bomb Iraq. We watch the shock and awe, bursts of red and yellow against a grainy black and blue skyline.

My mother isn't sure about all this, and neither am I. It all feels a bit like the family stuff feels to me, like some detail is missing. I start to think this feeling of not knowing, of being treated like a child, must be the stuff adulthood is made of.

My mother finally lands a job managing quality control work at Disney's DVD division, but not much changes. She takes to her own housecoats in the evenings. At first it's the puffy diving jacket, with its fleece lining. The nylon shell swishing in and out of the back door every night. The kitchen smells like tobacco, and I yell when my mother leaves the back door open even a crack.

She is an impulsive buyer, so with the extra cash comes fluffy pink robes, cloud-patterned jersey frocks, silky satin coverings that cling to her body just right and hardly fall below her bottom. She acquires an arsenal of housecoats. One for every mood.

She becomes a fixture in the house, like a lamp or the sofa or the yellow table. Every night, without fail, she can be found standing on the deck in a robe, an overfilled ashtray beside her, a glass of wine in one hand, a cigarette in the other. Wobbling. Always, she is wobbling. Because we smoke together I can't write her off completely. Travis is

---

of that pony, the one my grandmother had on Bannockburn. Where my grandmother kept her ancestry research. The details of how she met my grandfather. At least she told my grandmother she was sorry for running away so long ago. At least they had those five short weeks.

her dealer and she lets us share pot with her so she has someone to talk to.

Some nights are fun. Some nights we play bad board games, get high, laugh together. Then the conversation devolves.

"I think your father is cheating on his girlfriend," she says. I am picking at the aluminum siding of the yellow table, which has begun to peel in the spot where I usually sit. "He tried to tell me on the phone that he's going to meet up with our old friend Jodie. He was... like... bragging about it. She's a disgusting scofflaw. I don't even know why I talk to him anymore."

"So don't," I say. And then for hours it's *haven't you had enough why do you try to control me my therapist says you are crushing me.*

That night, I throw my arms around her in the kitchen, hold her tightly. In whispers I try to bring her back, while she tries to wrestle herself free.

I say, "It's me. I love you, remember?"[71]

I turn sixteen. I get a job at a city outreach center so I can save up and have a car like all the sparkly girls. Travis also gets a job with the city, to keep occupied while I'm working. He works for the water department and pays a straight-edge kid at school to give him a bag of clean piss so he can pass his drug test. He rigs a whole system for this: a contraption that holds the piss bag and a heating pad against his leg, inside his loose jeans. He has been caught smoking in his

---

71 For years she had dreams she was on the phone again, sitting on her bed in The House with the Red Door. I am sitting there with her, watching her. She is on the phone and she is fighting with my grandmother, trying to make her understand. My grandmother is saying, "I just can't believe my own son would lie to me and try to hurt you and I know you're trying but maybe not hard enough, Elizabeth. Maybe you can try harder, Elizabeth." On and on. And then my grandfather gets on the phone. He says, "Yes maybe if you only tried a little bit harder, Elizabeth." And my mother says in the dream, "Hey aren't you, uh, dead?" And she wakes up and feels that fear again, all over her bed sheets. Her heart aflutter and body just rattling, she thinks *no no please I don't want to feel that anymore I'm not that person anymore.*

bus on school grounds before, and has to see a probation officer, in the same outreach center, every month to take these tests. He lets me use this contraption for my drug test too, because he tells my mother and me that the drug test drinks never work for him, and they taste awful. I take the test in a private facility near the Burbank Airport and my heart surges while I'm in the bathroom transferring an unknown girl's piss from baggie to jar. My mother rejoices with us when our tests come back clean.

I work afternoons and sneak in stoned-sleepy every day, avoiding small talk whenever possible. I play the victim at this job. I tell my boss, who counsels kids my age with drug and family problems, all about my mother. I make myself out to be a survivor. I have perfect grades and here I am working at this adult job. My boss takes me under her wing. She has bright red curly hair that hangs around her face, short and cropped and thinning. All around her office are pictures of her riding horses. I know she is married but there are no pictures of her husband, no pictures of children.

It's not until I come into her office to ask about filing and find her crying at her desk that I learn why she goes home so late.

"Should I leave?" I say.

"No, please stay," she says. And she cries harder. "I'm going through a divorce and it's all my fault."

I hug her and think of myself the way I imagine she thinks of me. Like someone who needs her. I like the idea of stuffing myself into an identity other people can understand. It helps me forget about the office supplies I steal every day, how timid my phone-answering voice is, how ordinary home is beginning to feel.

After a few months on the job, my red-haired boss nominates me for a community award. It is called the Superstar award, and is given to teens who have overcome hard times. She tells the committee I am a great writer, because she has read some of my essays for English class. She tells me I should think about writing for a living, and I think this sounds like some sort of mystical job that nobody actually gets to do.

I win the award and have to give an interview. They film this interview in the photography lab at school. I am stoned, and class is in session while I am lit and positioned. Students scowl. I don't feel like a Superstar at all.

My mother has stopped going to meetings, so I start.

My boss at the outreach center recommends I go when I tell her that my mother thinks I have *control issues*. I tell her all about the other night, when we erupted in anger. My mother was hiding wine bottles in her room again while Travis cooked lamb shanks, which my mother had asked him to cook. I thought we were going to have a calm sober night with our lamb shanks so I made a cheesecake, but I when I saw the double bottle on her dresser I knew I was wrong. It was another battle of wants and needs. Of the wrong and right ways to mother.

Travis and I got into his van and drove up the 5 to Gorman, a deserted camping town just north of the Grapevine. We ate at a Flying J truck stop and I vented into my grilled cheese. We parked off of a dark road, near some trees, because we couldn't get into a proper campground. We lit up a joint and sprawled out in the icy backseat of his van. We had too few blankets. We hadn't planned the escape well.

I hardly slept, thinking of how my mother said that she *needed* the wine. "It's just so I can sleep," she always said. This looped in my head, along with the thought that I might be developing insomnia too.

"They will help you let go of responsibility," my boss says of the meetings. I like the idea of giving up more responsibility, so I take her advice.

The meetings are held down the street from The House with the Red Door, in a classroom in a little white chapel called The Little White Chapel. I only go twice, and the first time I drag Travis along. Being high at a meeting for the suffering children of addicts is uncomfortable. I feel like a hypocrite, but I don't think of my mother as an alcoholic, don't think of her as anything that simple really.

I eat cupcakes and Doritos in the corner, wait for everyone to sit down and get it over with already. I won't look at Travis. I admire all the funny little things on the wall. One picture that really gets me is this drawing of a little stick figure girl and her stick figure parents. They are all smiling like crazy and standing in front of their orange and blue house with the sun shining and a beach in the background. The piece is titled *Beach House*. It's sitting there on the big bulletin board of pictures, and I think it must be the most beautiful and depressing piece of art I have ever seen. I cannot understand how the Alateen organizers think that this kind of room is appropriate for a bunch of broken teenagers.

I watch my mother throw up, and the next morning before school I find her coffee cup filled with 99 Bananas. I feel like it's time to wallow with other people again. It's been a few weeks since the first meeting. I go because I want to make what has happened a big deal. Maybe it is a big deal. I am tapping into some kind of opportunity, trying to send her a message.

I go alone this second time, but I sit in the same spot. The leader interrupts my eating and picture-gazing, says something to me about moving into the circle. I hate her for calling me out, but I move into a chair anyway. She seems to be about my age, which makes things worse. She has frizzy blonde hair and a speckled complexion, and she is quite the chatterbox. She is serious and somber, then frantically happy when a weighty subject isn't being discussed.

I don't feel like I fit in with these people who are praying and sharing. I don't think it's what I need. I know now how my mother felt at AA meetings, and for the first time I understand why she has gone and stopped going so many times. These people are on some sort of drug too, always talking about a higher power and holding hands and crying. It frightens me that I always seem to see my mother's side of things.

"Do you know why we put the chairs in a circle?" the leader asks in the middle of some sort of lecture. People smile. Some nervously, some with so much confidence I think they are either stupid, or high like me.

I say probably so everyone can see each other, and then my face grows pink because I didn't expect to speak at all. The leader woman laughs and I want to leave.

"Okaaaayyyy, yes," she says, pauses. "It's actually to symbolize the cycle of dealing with addiction. Dealing with the disease is something that never ends."

I never want to go back to another meeting.

• • •

When my mother begins seeing Randy, a married man she meets at her new job at Disney, fresh robes flood in. More body-clinging robes, swimsuit covers made of terrycloth, even one fashioned like a kimono. The kimono robe is black with gold lapels, white orchids stitched all over it. When no one is around, I put the kimono on, feeling sexy.

I find sex toys hidden in the house. Edible everything. Battery-operated everything. Randy sleeps over most nights. He is still married. My mother drinks to the slurring point, and Travis and I smoke with the new couple, watch them disappear into the bedroom.

My mother has a fireplace in her room, and the smell of burning wood fills the house every night. She never starts the fire herself, always asks Travis or Randy to do it, and this becomes a new pet peeve of mine. She's keen on being weak now, always trying to float around in her robe.

I'm on a never-ending double date with my mother.

I rarely feel aroused anymore, although Travis still tries. I picture—with the most pressing repulsion—wild sexual acts taking place next to that fire. I often hear moaning, creaking, grunting. I tell Travis that I am too high and overwrought from the day and I have no sexual appetite, and he comforts me. He only wants to make me happy. I can see it in his eyes.

After an hour or so passes my mother and Randy re-emerge, haggard and worn. I feel so much turmoil watching Randy head for the door and drive off, back to his real family. Looking at my mother's face, before she has poured a refresher glass, I can tell she feels it too.[72]

We buy a new puppy after my mother begins making money, to make things feel okay. As a distraction from the legal mess my mother is dealing with, a mess I still can't follow.

Every night we blow smoke rings into the tiny Collie's muzzle, watch it stumble around and lap up water vigorously. She is a purebred and comes with a family tree, a long line of dog show winners.

"Good blood," my mother says, "just like us."

Travis is cooking pasta, furiously chopping onions and tomatoes and garlic. Salting water and browning meat, whipping his arms around and placing each chopped pile in a tiny bowl. My mother has purchased every cooking utensil he could ever want.

"Check out my *mise en place*," he says to me. We've been watching The Food Network, so we set everything up before we cook now. I kiss his cheek.

When everything is done, my mother refuses to sit down. She is all worry because Randy is not answering her calls. Or she has received new legal papers in the mail. Or she fought with her boss earlier at work. "Those stupid men think that because I'm a woman I don't know what I'm doing. Don't they know how long I've worked in this town?"

I raise my voice, tell her she's a drunk. Tell her she's a bad mother.

I have been to a few short therapy sessions of my own recently, another recommendation from my boss. I sit bi-weekly on a couch with an old woman with a puff of blonde hair and cry, whine. I like

72 She would say she was only trying to get on with her life.

to talk to her. I like to talk. I like to recount my bad days and hear her tell me new ways to think of them. She helps me rewrite these bits of my life, though I always leave with a sense that there is more to rewrite.

A few weeks ago, she hypnotized me. I was preparing to take the SATs, and she told me to imagine a pencil in my hand. I was high, always am, so even though I knew I wasn't in any sort of trance, I was with her. She said I should imagine all of my potential pouring into that pencil, imagine everything I have coming out of it, and I felt something rushing into my pinched fingertips, but it didn't feel like potential.

My therapist says that when you don't understand something you often feel as though you must destroy that thing. I know there's more to it than that. When you don't understand something—and you have no ability to change it, and it's there every day in your face—you have to destroy *something*. You have to destroy to remind yourself that you can still affect the world around you.

I scream at my mother until my throat goes dry. I start coughing so hard that I have to go to the toilet to puke. She has to vomit too so we both throw up at the same time, in different bathrooms.

I am perpetually wringing out a wet cloth, trying to expel something.[73]

---

73 She had an image she made up with the help of her favorite therapist, a woman who worked in the Valley. She would say it's important to share because it says something about her, about her will to live, about how no matter what, she never gave up loving her daughters. This visualization was the only way she was able to stop drinking in those days without AA or medication. The therapist told her to dream up the most peaceful image she could think of, to call it to mind any time she felt like she was on the brink of breaking down. Somewhere along the way she must have lost the ability to call the image up. This is what she thought of: she was riding on a huge golden-feathered goose like Mother Goose herself, could feel her feathers and her muscles moving if she really concentrated; it sounds silly but she would break through Cloud Nine, where we used to meet in our dreams; she would break through this beautiful fluffy cloud and it was all blue sky, no one anywhere around, and all those feelings that she wasn't good enough, that

• • •

When summer hits, my mother whittles down to skin and bones. This makes her feel sexy, young. She runs a triathlon sponsored by Disney, and she jogs with Mickey Mouse ears pinned to the paper number that covers her fragile shoulder blades. Her skinny legs, all bone and muscle. I am proud of her as I watch her break the finish line on a sour, grey morning in Redondo Beach. The waves are crashing and I think for a moment that she might be getting her life together.

But soon I realize she has stopped eating. That she eats only late into the night now, after she has been drinking. When my sister comes to visit for the holidays she goes on and on about how skinny my mother and I are. This is the first time I realize that I too look emaciated. The pot doesn't make me hungry anymore, just makes me feel evened out. We never eat breakfast, and I skip lunch to hot-box Travis's car. He still cooks for us some nights, but we only pick at our food.

She acquires a pill for everything. She is taking Ambien now, but she will try yet another brand of sleeping pills when she tries another new psychiatrist. She also takes pills for her anxiety, and pills for her shakes.[74]

---

she would never be good enough, all of those feelings dissipated, broke up with the cotton of the cloud; and on the horizon she could see these tiny babies, playing with toys on the crest of the sun, and she knew they were her unborn grandchildren; and every time the image came she would just weep with this feeling of timelessness, this feeling of flying into this completely light unburdened space.

74 The truth is that her therapists were all digging up her past. They wanted to talk about her father and her mother and her anger towards her brother and sisters and this only made things worse. But she did realize things she had never realized before. She did realize that ever since she ran away she felt that God had left her, so she had given up on God the way he had given up on her.

They prescribed new medications for everything, every time she had a

She hasn't been to a general practitioner in years, and tells me she fears her heart is acting up again, though she says it's hard to tell if it's arrhythmia or overwhelm.

During the day I lay by the pool with the few girlfriends I have left and Travis gets us high. Sometimes we smoke cigarettes or make guacamole with California avocados and we feel lucky. Travis buys turntables and stores them in my room, spins and scratches records all day because he thinks he might want to be a DJ.

I stay in the sun all day because I have been taught that to be tan is to be pretty. I have the same pale skin as my mother, though I stay in denial about this just like she always has. I rub oil all over my body. She tells me again and again that she used to use baby oil in Hancock Park. My chest, cleavage to collarbone, ripens and dimples in the sun.

On the weekends, we occasionally throw parties, like we used to in The Electrical Flat. My mother buys loads of food and drinks and lets me have anyone I want over. I rekindle some friendships. Mostly I smoke at these parties, already afraid to drink like my mother, to make it too easy for anyone to compare us.

The morning after these parties, when The House with the Red Door is overrun with bottles, cans, stickiness, she always says pleadingly, "It was fun, wasn't it?"

I leave a mess in the backyard. Pool towels left out, the new lounge chairs moved all over the newly painted deck. My mother has been inside in her bikini most of the day drinking wine. She erupts when she sees how I have left the backyard, and the back-and-forth ends when I slam our new puppy's paw in the backdoor by mistake. The whimper is deathly, and techno music reverberates over and under it.

---

breakdown. She felt it getting out of control but they were so convincing, telling her that she was bipolar and manic and then just sleep-deprived, and any answer sounded like one she should take. Any answer sounded plausible.

My mother never lets me forget the incident. She pays Travis to take the puppy to the vet, since she isn't in a state to drive, and as we're leaving she tells me that she worries that I might be *naturally violent*. She reminds me that when I was very young, I slammed a door when I was fighting with her and, tracing my finger absentmindedly along the door as it flew shut, I caught a finger in the hinge, crushed it.

I look at the little dip in my cuticle, an oddly recessed border between finger and nail. I look down and think that I have always wanted something more from her, and have always wanted to get closer to her than was possible.[75]

Noon on a Saturday. A commercial for cell phones or phone service is on. Mick Jagger is dancing across the stage flapping his arms like a bird, singing about how he *can't get no satisfaction* from his phone company. My mother is in front of the TV, a glass of white wine in her hand. She is connected with Mick, as though they share a secret. She bounces around like a baby in a crib and her eyes are glossy, her facial muscles relaxed, her body sort of bucking.

"Man, I remember those days," she says as it ends.

I walk into this scene repeatedly. I always shoot her a look, try to make her feel pathetic, and she stops her bouncing, walks slowly outside with her drink, her eyes set deep in thought, maybe about herself, maybe about me. You can never be too sure when she's like this. You can see behind her glances that she isn't staying with thoughts too long. A song or a joke on television or something like that Mick Jagger commercial always gets to her though, makes her feel nostalgic.

I think of how I used to sit with my mother while she sip-sipped in the red living room, on the stiff and stylish loveseat, and she would ask me if I could guess which celebrity spoke the voiceover on each commercial. I hated this game, but became an expert quickly

75 She would say she knew I had been unhappy, but she never knew I had felt so alone.

and played along almost without intending to.

I take a shower, which I often do when she disappears like this. Let the heat of the water strip me of everything, all of the energy in my body dropping out. My face runs off and away, down the drain with the water. I open my eyes, wanting to feel the pressurized water blind me. It feels terrible, the scorching water, but it feels like it's taking something out of me.

My mother does this too. Takes baths and showers too hot.

I imagine I'm a director. I shoot a scene with my mother and I both sweating in separate bathtubs, only a wall between us.

The bathroom smells like plastic and baby powder. It's from the rubber ducks we decorated with, but it makes me think of Cabbage Patch Dolls. Makes me wonder whether they were plush or hard plastic like Barbie dolls but I can't remember. Makes me think of last night, when Travis and I snorted Special K in my room and hardened, immobile for hours. We showered when we could finally move and put the ducks between our legs and humped each other and called it *ducking*. We thought it was funny but now it makes me feel sick. I have never thought of myself as someone who could snort something.

My nose feels larger, more visible, because of it.

I sit on the toilet, wonder how much longer Travis will be out on runs. He is selling pot to schoolmates now. I look out the bathroom window, can't spot my mother on the deck. I wonder if she is already asleep, or trying to read a book through her wine eyes. I squint and the sunlight blurs and everything seems to be long lines of color, light just reaching for me.[76]

The towel is rough and worn-in at the same time, from too much bleaching and washing and forgetting the fabric softener. I am

76 It wasn't as if she didn't know she was losing her handle on things, but what was she supposed to do? For years she regretted that pages of novels, which she read in a haze at the time, were lost to her. Whole plotlines left spotty in her mind from the late hours she spent trying to read what the authors were saying, trying to straighten out the typography.

wondering how this can be, how it can feel like two textures.

She loves to clean. "When in doubt, throw bleach on it," she always says. Tomorrow, if it's Sunday, she will listen to Judy Collins and clean all day. She will time it so she can sip wine through it, then find herself drunk and sleepy just when everything is in order.

I think of how she used to warm these towels for me, wrap me up from behind.[77]

I am in the bathroom cooling off when I hear it. A loud thump. I think it might be my mother, and something in me wants it to be her, wants her to be injured, wants this to be the moment that moves something in her.

I hear her sobbing in the kitchen.

In my towel I find her there, on the floor, a broken glass in one hand, wine spilled across the linoleum, her knee seeping blood. She looks up and her face turns into a smile and a laugh and she tries to pretend as though the glass and the wine and the blood are not there at all.

"Hi," she says, but it comes out *hiiiiiieeee*. "I didn't know you were still here."

She tries to stand up but her legs crumple beneath her, and she hits her knee hard again on the floor and lets out a little yelp.

I want to go to her and pick her up but I am frozen, watching her, fixing my towel. I want to take her in my arms and tell her it isn't so bad, life isn't so bad, she's such a good mother, but I just stand there.

"Are you okay?" I say.

"Oh, angel baby, it's so good of you to *care*," she says.

She grapples for the counter and stands up. She turns, tugging her silk robe closed, scanning the room for nothing in particular, on the verge of some great thought. She swallows hard, and I can hear

---

77 She would say that those days were not the first time she thought about suicide. They also weren't the last. She felt so alone, so useless, so bored with life, but she couldn't think of what to do to get out of the hole.

her dry lips and mouth sticking.

Do I busy myself with something? Mail on the yellow table? Do I get a snack? Or do I just stand, watching her? I look past the kitchen, down the hall and into her room where the TV is glowing. She is watching The History Channel.

She is only that broken skin for the moment, only that fragile knee. I don't know this part of her body, like I know the rest.[78]

"Are you okay?" I say.

"Do you know what I realized today?" she says. "What my therapist helped me realize? There's nothing… *special* about me."

• • •

We decide it could be fun to capitalize on our habits. So we mail order weed seeds, the finest we can find. For days Travis and my mother fold seedlings into damp paper towels, wait for them to sprout.

All summer my mother has been drunkenly tilling the garden past the wooden deck. We nestle the first seedling that sprouts a root into the dirt behind the tomato and strawberry plants, the plants we are still trying to revive, even though the rats have eaten up their fruit. Travis takes it all on like a project. He pisses in cups and mixes the piss with fertilizer, pours the solution all over the plant because he reads *High Times*. My mother and I splay out on lounge chairs in our bikinis and watch him work.

The plant grows slowly but when it starts budding it's like emerald crystals blinking in the sun.

Travis and I are on the bluff of some kind of adulthood.

One night, I smash a window while fighting with him. He begins to pull out of the driveway in anger while I am telling him that he is

78 She would, of course, have to say, at some point, that I chose to take my clothes off and stand naked in front of the world. I chose to tell my story, but she did not.

too weak, that he never stands up for himself.

"You are just like your father," I say.

And he says, "You are just like your mother."

I slam my flat hand against the front window, the one right next to the red door. I hit it with everything in me, and the glass fissures all over.

This sort of thing must always happen when two people love each other as much as we do, I think.

It's after sundown, when our arguments usually erupt. When we can yell in the streets and feel like everything we do is unhinged and unstoppable. My mother doesn't hear the break somehow, doesn't come out of her room and walk to buy more wine because she is worried for us, the way she usually does when we argue. But she sees the cracks in the window the next morning, and we play dumb.

"It had to be my brother," she says. "He's trying to make it look like I can't be trusted. Do you think he's snapping pictures of us?"

With the big plant budding in the backyard, her paranoia has begun to multiply.

"Or someone is trying to break in to steal the plant," she says. "Who have you told?"

One of her late nights tips the scale, and just weeks before it's time to harvest, my mother comes into my bedroom and tells Travis we have to uproot the plant. She says it's too much of a risk, she says she thinks it was a bad idea. She says it can't wait, her voice all Ambien and wine.

In the dark she holds a wavering flashlight above us, sipping white wine. We carefully fondle the roots, nursing them out of the soil. She weeps over us a little, feeling guilty, apologizing. I miss school the next day so that we can drive the plant over to a friend's garage, where we set up lights and an indoor fan to keep it cool. Despite our best efforts, it wilts slowly over the next few days.

Just before Halloween, some kids leave a flaming bag of shit on our doorstep. She is sure someone is out to get her. Every time we hear a helicopter chopping overhead, likely spotlighting some backyard keg party, she thinks it's coming for us. She says we can't have parties anymore, it's too much of a risk.

I string my own neon bead bracelets, put on yellow Dickies. I make a shirt out of felt and my mother stitches me in tight. I read that ecstasy was originally used in clinical settings, to remind PTSD sufferers and severe depressives what it feels like to be happy. This excites me. I can frame my night as therapeutic.

The first time it hits me, I'm standing in line outside of a club in a strip mall in Riverside, and I feel my body sink into itself. That night I get lost in the crowd, and find Travis in a room that appears to function as a bowling alley during the day. His pupils are black and big like buttons, and he says *baybeeee* when he sees me and holds me with such warmth, such softness. He gives me menthol this and that and has a girl wave lights in my face. He rubs my shoulders, tells me what the LSD is making him see. He says I am a window, a melty window. He is all eyes. Cave eyes, holes of eyes. But I am swimming in soft glue, my skin boundless.

He has taken these colored tabs before. I have not, and don't want to. I want only to be happy like this. Girls I don't know stroke my arms and christen me with plastic bracelets, kiss my cheeks. We are all moist-armed, faces glowing. We climb onto a rafter at some point and I see myself falling, flying. When we climb down, we ascend into a circle of squirming kissing bodies.

I want him to be a good dancer. I know this as he moves in the crowd, his legs like scissors, stomping and hopping. I could love a good dancer.

So we move this way all night and my hair gets spongy with sweat. When we walk to the car I am falling onto him, pressing my back into him, my eyes blinking closed I feel so good, sucking on a pacifier. I think of how my mother let me suck on a pacifier until I was six, and then just before the divorce, took it away from me, told me it was lost.

"I sucked my thumb 'til I was ten," I say. The sun is coming up, but the car has been broken into. The stereo is gone. Travis scoops glass from my seat, from his seat, and then holds his hands up in front of his face. They are bleeding a little bit all over. I laugh and he makes a huge O face, both of us nearly falling back, in slow motion.

Travis gets us home, and I'm in awe of his abilities, driving in such a state. He says the acid makes him a better driver. When we get there, the driveway is dripping, the grass underneath the willow tree swollen with water. I know my mother is likely awake. She has left the sprinklers on again for hours, after getting caught up drinking. As we walk through the red door, and I see that the lights are on, I am happy that I will get to spend time with her, will get to prattle on about the night. I am happy because I know she will say, "Tell me every little *detail*!"

We smoke from the bong with her and talk at the yellow table and my chest is warm, like at a good holiday dinner. I tell her the kids at these things are like new hippies, they're into peace and unity.

"Your father and I marched on MacArthur Park in '72," she says. "There were *tons* of people there. We felt so out of place, being *so* young—everyone else was in their twenties or thirties and had the perfect hippie outfits and I was *barely* eighteen—but I knew I would *never* forget being there, with the L.A. skyline staring down at us, everyone shouting and singing. I can't imagine there being anything like that time ever again."

We have brought a moneyed drug pal back with us, a high school boy who buys from Travis, and he has brought a packet of white dust from the club, a packet he found on the floor in the bathroom. I've never seen this kind of powder before, but I know what it is.

My mother brings her beautiful vanity mirror out from her bedroom, the one with the cherry wood frame. She lays it on the yellow table. She hovers over the mirror and fashions a line, watching herself, not the powder, as she does this. I watch my mother and the moneyed guy do a line while I abstain. She leans over, sniffs it up, and her body opens up. Her body like a well, something I fall into.[79]

I look out the kitchen window in my haze, thinking that something is not right, something is certainly not right.[80]

I look to where the plant used to be. Now, only a hole. The pool is growing sour, beginning to carpet and breathe with algae.[81] The wood planks of the deck are beginning to warp, cigarettes are piling

---

79 And yet, her character is so unbecoming, there's nothing redeeming about her—can't I write a scene that shows the times when she was a good mother?

80 Wouldn't it be better to write about the good times? Wouldn't it be better to spend more time writing about her father's successes, the days her mother and father spent in New York at the 21 Club, the Hancock Park house, and all the lazy summer days she spent by the pool with her siblings? The time my grandmother dressed my mother and her twin sister in frills, gave them barrettes, and then took them to Los Angeles Country Club, pushed them forward right smack into JFK, and said there's the president shake his hand girls, before the Marilyn scandal, when he was such an awe-inspiring man, and he said to them why hello so politely, even though the club was a Republican enclave and was only being used for landing purposes? The way she used to braid my hair with ribbons and later how she blow-dried it every morning for me, even though I cried because it hurt and it took so long, because I wanted my hair in the same smooth style she wore hers? Couldn't I focus more on her career, how much she once meant to people in Hollywood, how much they used to appreciate her, and how she climbed the ladder without any education or training, just with her own personality, a woman in an aggressive male world? Couldn't I show the way I loved her even when our relationship became a bit too close, a bit untraditional? The vacation we took to Ojai, when we got high out of our minds and giggled at the waitress who told us we had to finish our lamb shanks before we were allowed to order dessert?

81 She would ask, didn't I ever like the time we spent together? Weren't those days in some fucked up way wonderful parts of our lives? A time when we really knew each other, in all of our raw failure?

up in a wet trashcan.[82] My mother stands, begins a little dance.[83]

---

82 She would not want to relive the night in downtown L.A. She must have wanted to tag along, though it's possible that we may have invited her, because I did like having her around sometimes. She took that pill and felt so alive and we danced and I didn't make fun of her—but then, oh God maybe it isn't a redemptive story at all. Quite suddenly it overtook her and all she felt was strung out. It wasn't what she expected and not how I had described it at all, so it must not have been the best. She knew this right away. She had worried about her heart, feeling it flutter inside her chest. She had worried that the arrhythmia would get out of control if there was speed in the pills. She had worried that her heart would stop altogether.
Then she lost me and found herself dancing with this older Asian man and he took her off into this hallway that was on the side of the club where the rave was. It didn't take long for her to realize it was some sort of opium hideout. She probably should have been scared and she knew it but she just started laughing. Eventually she left to find me but somewhere in there roaming around that club with the lights, and kids with glow sticks and furry pants, it hit her where she was, and that she was with me, she was with her daughter, and then she started crying. She sat down by a speaker because the thud of the music at least felt nice and her heart was feeling light now but she could not stop crying. So many girls my age were looking and pointing at her, as she clung to herself, just hoping I wouldn't find her yet, just hoping she could find a way to pull herself together.

83 She would say that the truth is that I don't even know the half of it. That the real ugliness is harder to share than I might think, and had nothing to do with me, happened after I left when she found herself all alone in that house. She would say though, that if I really think it's important, if I'm sure I want to know the truth, even though she doesn't see what good will come of it, she will tell me.

PART THREE

amanda MONTEI

THE TENDERLOIN STUDIO

When my mother's older sister left the apartment on Irving for Manhattan Beach, my grandfather said to her, "You can't solve all of your problems by leaving."

And she said, "Yes I can."

Our family lived by this credo. And so, two days after I graduated high school, I left with Travis for San Francisco. I left for new walls, new pleasures, a new life. My mother stayed behind, alone for the first time in over thirty years.

"I'm just so afraid you're going to run off and get married and make all the same mistakes that I did because you think you hate your mother," she said, holding my hand unsteadily through the U-Haul window before we pulled away.

She never let me forget her days as a runaway. The way she remembered it, I had been threatening to leave for years. What should have seemed like a rite of passage, felt to her, and so to me, like abandonment. She seemed to have forgotten how many times over the past two years she had suggested that I find another place to live.

"I will never make the same mistakes you did," I said to her, as I moved to roll up the window. She nodded her head. She was as droopy as the weeping willow behind her. It was clearly not the goodbye conversation she had pictured.

On my lap were the pins that went to me when my grandmother died. A brown wooden box the shape of a church window. Velvet blue lining, the entire façade a door. Bread-box size in reality, years-big in my mind. Inside were pins from various organizations. Daughters of the American Revolution, Dames of the Magna Carta. This was not an inheritance. I was to hide the pins from the rest of the family, my mother told me, in a closet in my new apartment, high up, behind stored hats and bags. She handed them to me just before we drove away, told me as she had before that I am also a member of these organizations. Maybe I could get a scholarship from one of them.

She said, "Once you're in, you're in!" What if I don't want to be in?

As we pulled out of the driveway, she crooked each finger in her right hand, made The Claw and bounced her forearm up and down—our family wave. She had tears in her eyes, and I watched her, through the side mirror, as she attempted composure, and walked back through the red door. Then I said to Travis, "We're off!"

We drove up the coast, took Highway One, and smoked our way to San Francisco in the U-Haul, stopping to look at scenic points. We could become nature lovers, we decided, and took in vistas.

When we arrived at our apartment for the first time, we ran upstairs and christened the studio with our bongs and pipes. After we finished, we skipped happily out to the curb, only to find that the U-Haul was gone. It had been towed to a lot in the Mission.[84]

I don't remember when I fell in love with Travis, though I guess you never do. Our love was like an ocean shelf that way. One minute I was walking on it so steadily, and the next thing I knew the bottom

84 She felt so lost. Her girls were gone and her mother was gone and her family—gone. What did she have? She had a job, finally, yes. She cried so hard when that stupid U-Haul pulled away. She thought I would never forgive her for all she put me through. The house was so quiet and all she could think about was whether or not her daughters still loved her, if they would ever love her again. Whether her twin sister thought of her when she looked in the mirror. Whether she thought of her breathing, walking, styling her hair.

She did have Randy but all they did was have sex, which was nice for a change, though after a while the niceness wore off, and it turned into a kind of pain. She stayed up nights wondering is this what love is supposed to feel like? She knew she was in a downward spiral, but that's how those things go. She would just get a little more gone, and everything felt better. Even in that haze all she could think was, *My God I'm like my mother with her Milltowns, like my father with his beer, my God I'm like my father.*

had dropped out from under me and I was eye-deep in something that was pushing me every which way, pulling me further out, and there was nowhere for me to catch my footing.

I suppose I could say I was young, that I didn't know anything about love, though I suspected even then that love is a constant discovering. Still, I knew that I would never marry him. I could never picture our children. I thought that all that collapsing, all that painful merging, was what love was supposed to feel like. It took a long time to realize that this was not the truth.

We moved in together because he wanted to, and I wanted to get away from my mother. I had a good reason to say yes and be in love with love. He went to cooking school and I went to college. He came home smelling warm and salty, finger condoms harboring cuts, hands puckered from vinegars. He cooked something new for me late every night with the fervor of a child piecing the world together. We stopped going dancing, stopped going out, so I tried to think of him as a culinary artist, and this worked for a while.

We rented an apartment in the Tenderloin, a sixth-floor studio, in the Pontchatrain apartments on the corner of Geary and Leavenworth. We portioned off a makeshift office with a Chinese room divider. We bought a wicker round chair that was never comfortable. We slept on a futon that doubled as a couch during the day, which I complained about setting up and breaking down each morning and night.

Our kitchen was awkward and small, and the window looked right into our neighbors' window, where the matriarch hung fish to dry. Smoking one night on the roof, we discovered that she hung fish to dry there, too. Later, I would hide on that roof, needing to get away, when Travis and my arguments became furious again.

When we got home after long days, we sang *Pontchartraaain, oh darling Pontchartraaain* to the tune of "Danke Shoen." We got high in that little dingy apartment every night, ate bags of fresh ciabatta from the Ferry Plaza Farmer's Market, with the greenest olive oil we could find. Slipper bread, he told me. That's how it translated. He pretended the bread was a shoe, held it up to my foot, and said he had found his Cinderella.

I spoke to my mother on the phone most nights in our tiny apartment, sitting on the fire escape smoking from a small water pipe, listening to the sounds of people yelling in the streets. I told her about every single thing I did every day because that was the sort of thing you do on the phone with your mother as you're learning to be a grown-up.

I told her about the time Travis hit a fevered man with his motorized scooter.

He came home yelling, "I hit a *crack head*!" A huge grin on his face, blood on his shirt, laughing. He told me that the policemen had apologized to him and said that this sort of thing happened in our neighborhood at least once a month. I told my mother this the next day, when Travis was away at cooking school. I said I couldn't understand this sort of apology and couldn't understand how someone could laugh with blood on his shirt like that. I told her that I wanted to find that poor man and tell him that I didn't think his life was such a joke.

"Oh, how awful," she would say. "Travis must have been in shock."

I wasn't sure who she was siding with.

Whenever my mother spoke back to me, I listened for the drunk lilt in her voice.

Often she said things like, "I bought a sushi maker!" There were always new products she had ordered late at night or bought in checkout lines. I scolded her for these purchases, telling her that she was a sucker.

"That's why they have sales," I said. "To trick you."

It seemed she bought up everything that was on sale all the time, and then she'd go on about how she couldn't make the bills because she wasn't getting paid enough. It felt like the hardest thing in the world, to try to explain the work that stores were doing on her.

Of course, after a while, there were also many things that I kept from her.

I didn't tell her about the night I finally decided I was ready to try LSD. I had always avoided it, for fear that I had inherited my mother's weak heart. Now I felt built up by the city, stronger. And so we took the buses out to Haight and Stanyan and ventured into Golden Gate Park, walking through a damp tunnel where a guy in wide old JNCO jeans was whipping the ankles of another other guy with a long chain. Travis picked someone out, wasn't convinced, and then asked a stereotypically hippie-looking girl.

Back in the apartment, we each took two of the tabs. They had little mouths on them. And of course they worked, too well. The chest of drawers we had bought at a used furniture shop, the one with gold and white paint and swirly carvings, breathed in my direction, and I felt we should remove our clothes, open all the blinds. We had tall windows, it was one thing we liked about the apartment. We could look up at the penthouses in the buildings around us and imagine what the well-off were doing, how one day we would do the same things. We could make out the bay if we looked up Leavenworth, up and over the steep hill that was the striking separation between Nob Hill and us.

The openness was too much for me, so I demanded that we shut the blinds, put all of our clothes back on, and take a walk. I was all panic, thinking about my mother's heart, thinking about my own heart beating out of my chest, what that might look like, might feel like. Thinking about what my mother used to say about *control issues*. I felt it now, that desire to own my body, own the world, to believe in an unquestionable order of things.

We walked down Geary towards Union Square, past the Hotel California, which made Travis get wide-eyed, because his father had loved the Eagles. Was this *the* Hotel California? Past the Hotel Monaco with its silly bellman on the curb at all hours, smiling goofily with that cap. What do you call a cap like that? Up to the Clift Hotel, which pulsed with the sounds of the The Redwood Room, the nightclub we had heard about, and Asia de Cuba, the bougie restaurant my mother was always telling me to *check out*, because she frequented the one at the top of the Mondrian on Sunset when her businesses were doing well. There were women in furs lined up, men in penny loafers. I looked down, and realized I was wearing hazard-orange sweatpants, which I usually only wore around the house. That's when I spun into myself.

We bolted off into an alley and I tried to breathe, but the image of my mother before the TV came to me, as it had so many times before. I could never shake that vision of my mother crying for strangers. Standing there sobbing, after what? September 11? After a white girl was found raped and murdered? After an epic natural disaster? The vision was just a memory, so it was often something I retooled. In any case, her empathy had always seemed wrong, useless.

Now, I could feel how her heart must have felt all the time. There was so much tenuousness in the world, so much chafing.[85]

I huddled around myself, crouched down in that alley in my stupid orange pants, and Travis stroked my shoulders.

I waited.

• • •

I dove into self-help books. I used to get really high with Travis and tell him timidly about how much anxiety I had. Speaking, it was

85 She is in the house alone. Months after I've left. Randy has gone back to his wife. He told my mother before he left that he would *have the divorce talk finally*, and she is outside on the deck drinking wine, trying to imagine the conversation he will have. She can't. He is always saying that he is about to leave his wife. He is always saying that my mother is the only one for him. Why does she believe him? Every day she thinks she should tell him never to call her again, but something tells her to hold out, tells her he will be hers fully soon. If she can just hold on, if she can just give enough of herself, he will see that she deserves to be loved by him. She smokes on that deck all night, thinking that she must have done something terribly wrong to deserve all the shit that happens to her. She wishes that her daughters would stop telling her on the phone that everyone thinks this way, because it only makes her feel worse.

such a rush of relief, my chest opened up. I found a book that made me do this whole process where I'd have to say whether I felt above or below the line. The book called this procedure "doing cycles." The line indicated feeling good, feeling content. It wasn't advisable to be above or below the line, so that meant it wasn't advisable to feel too excited or unbearably happy. Whenever I felt elated, say from too much coffee, I thought I had inherited my mother's palpitations. Though I was usually below the line, and then I'd have to talk myself up. I'd have to slowly break apart the feeling. If I felt ugly, I'd have to break that into pieces. *Are my expectations reasonable? What is the essential pain? What is the earned reward?* I loved this, because it was like falling into a maze of words, where this plain old feeling had multiplied into tons of emotions and experiences the longer I sat with it. It felt comforting to know I could talk with myself in this very directed way.

The book also taught me that *more skills are needed in modern life*, and that *parents can't give skills they don't have*. On the phone, I told my mother that I understood this, that I understood her parents didn't have *skills* either. She bought the book the next day, and we both toted around pocket-sized cut-outs from the book, which reminded us how to do a cycle. The book suggested you keep a journal. My mother decorated a spiral notebook with scrapbooking flowers and mailed it to me.

Some nights, when I was nearing a panic attack, Travis sat beside me on our futon and broke apart feelings next to me. He held my hand. On my birthday that first year in San Francisco, he wrote me a note in the morning while I was still sleeping, before heading off to school. He promised me that when he got home, the first thing we would do was smoke a bowl and do cycles together.

Later, in the hospital, I wondered if I dragged him into my ugly world, if he stayed there.

I didn't drink in the Tenderloin apartment, but I still found myself weak and needy. I had never been a big drinker, besides the nights in The Electrical Flat, though I learned quickly, in college, that everyone is a drunk when they're young, and I wondered whether I had ever had any grounds to yell at my mother. The students in my classes would come in with such haggard faces, and boast about how awful they felt. Travis and I kept to ourselves, not understanding the desire to drink, and began smoking even more. We didn't want to fit in with any crowd. Not the cooks, not the commuting university students. We made excuses for why this might be: we had all we needed *right here*.[86]

I berated Travis often then, for everything and for nothing. "Do you know the sort of men I could have?" I'd say when he was getting high and I was trying to write papers. I saw them eyeing me at school, but chose to go home and do cycles and smoke pot instead.

---

86 Now that her children have left home, she has to move more children in. She can't believe it. She puts an ad in the paper—Two Rooms for Rent—what other choice does she have. The first woman who answers seems nice enough, but when my mother finds out she has a baby, she tells her it simply can't work. With her luck, the baby would find its way outside and she would come home after a long day at work, go outside to smoke a cigarette, and find a two year-old face down in the swimming pool. Which she can't even afford to keep clean anymore.

Is she being too picky? Perhaps.

She gets a response from a creepy older man who seems like he thinks he might get her to bed, if he can just get her to let him move in. She gets a call from a young girl who snaps her gum over the phone—classless. She interviews two young guys who seem to think they can talk her down on the price, because they're paying tuition at some community college in Glendale.

On the phone, I tell her that she shouldn't run the air conditioner so much after she tells me about the unmanageable electricity bills. She tries to explain that there is really no point in owning a home that one can't be comfortable in, and of course I don't understand what the house means to her, though she knows that I will someday. I tell her that she should give up the fight if she can't make the mortgage payments, that she should just get over the stigma of the word apartment, at least she is alive and healthy. Looking down at the yellow table, she flips through the litigation papers on the table. The title of the house had been put temporarily in both her name, and her mother's. Just for the first year, while my mother got back on her feet and found a job. Now that the time has come to transfer full ownership, her siblings have all called in lawyers.

I read a lot too, talked with my mother on the phone about how I was falling in love with reading. I tried to give Travis books, but he refused to read. He said it was boring.

I slowly became an insomniac, thinking about what a failed night of rest would bring the next day, but I refused to take pills for this, having seen how they only worsened her sleeplessness, and having been taught to fear all those orange bottles. I let my thoughts keep me up, and grew more cranky.

I wanted to get everything ugly out from inside me and give it to him. Some days, I told him I never wanted to smoke again, just wanted to be shiny and happy and ride bikes through Golden Gate Park. We bought bikes, but when we rode them high across the Golden Gate Bridge the wind knocked us against the safety fences and we yelled at each other, tired and worn and scared.

I didn't want to push Travis away, but I was receding. All I did was stay indoors, smoking and watching the Food Network, squinting at class assignments. I was pale. I cried to him in our suffocating apartment in the Tenderloin about the times I had fooled around with girls when I was little. I sobbed and shook and asked him if he thought it meant I had been denying something all my life. Everything about my girlhood haunted me. I haunted myself.

At school, I gathered up words and new ways of seeing the world. In a Sociology class I learned that culture is thrust upon us, and I realized I had been consuming my mother's culture my whole life. I learned about 'agency.' I learned that you know you've learned a language once it appears in your dreams. I had never had a nightmare that was not composed of mounting tension, of the imminence not of death, but of a total loss of self. Nightly I wondered what language did I actually speak?[87]

---

87 She wants so badly to have evenings to herself, doesn't want to worry anymore about what anyone thinks of her. She doesn't want to have to be "on" anymore. She has been "on" her whole life. She is dreading the new life she is about to stick herself with, one with strangers roaming in and out of her kitchen, but she does think on some level it may be nice to have a full

house again.

On the deck, smoking and sipping wine, she sometimes forgets that Randy is still married. He is living on his own now. She has dinner with his family. She reviews his divorce papers. And yet, most nights, she is alone. She tries to busy herself, often working overtime, trying to make ends meet. She feels as though I am cutting her out of my life and wonders if I'll ever come back to her.

amanda MONTEI

THE FLAT ON NINETEENTH AVENUE

In the Tenderloin, I wanted so badly to find something to love. I googled jobs every day, made five-year plans. My best plan was that we would become cheese makers. We bought books at the Ferry Building, spent free afternoons cheese tasting around the city. I fantasized about milking cows, walking green pastures every morning, and living a simple life. We learned about bacteria and aging processes. The whole endeavor was scientific *and* artful, and I thought that sort of balance was just what we needed to make us happy. But this dream wasn't enough. The tiny apartment in the Tenderloin still felt like it was closing in on us.

Travis and I moved to the Sunset after a year. It was a larger one bedroom apartment on Nineteenth Avenue with a separate living room, and a dining room, where we set up a used elementary school craft table. The place was a duplex, an older man lived in the flat below. The narrow backyard was neglected, so we asked to turn it into a vegetable garden. We tilled the dry sandy soil, set up a compost system to fortify it. When chard and squash and lettuces popped up, we bought a hibachi grill and made every meal down there, smoke overtaking nearby yards, covering up the smells of fish and fried food that always hung around the area.

Travis finished his program and landed a job at a budding upscale restaurant. We saved up money and had luxurious dinners at Gary Danko and other fancy cafes on Market. We ate pastries from Tartine, where I saw men reading *The New Yorker.* I told Travis I wanted to be the sort of couple that had habitual acts. So we drank espresso at Delores Park on Saturdays. We bought local everything and chomped on grass-fed beef sandwiches at the farmer's market on Sundays, the bay gulls hanging around hoping for a piece of our lunch. The new job brought new recipes, and when Travis was rubbing garlic and heirloom tomatoes onto toasted bread, when he was showing me what *gremolata* was, explaining the *mother sauces,* it felt like we were piecing a life together.

I was eating to avoid acknowledging how far apart Travis and I were.

On the phone one night, trying to figure out who I could be, I asked my mother why she had stopped working at the needlepoint store, where she worked after she ran away from home.

I said, "It seemed like your one passion. Your art."

She told me she got the job as a dare, and found the work dull and tedious. She said, laughing, "It was most certainly *not* something I loved! It was the worst time of my life!"[88]

He became like an ill-fitting shoe, that's why I left. He blistered me, and I him, only he never noticed it out loud. I took a graduate-level class on popular culture, and the course description had the word *jurisprudence* in it, was filled with students who knew all about Marx and the male gaze and capitalism. Just like that there were two of me. I had enrolled in the course not even knowing what *jurisprudence*

---

88 When the holidays are over, she is strapped. Should she miss a mortgage payment now, her siblings would only hold it against her. She commits to accepting the next person that answers her ad. She can't lose the only home that has ever been hers.

She gets two calls on the same day. A man and a woman. The woman, Vicky, comes through the house and loves my old wing. Her outfit is a little raunchy, but my mother feels she isn't in the place to judge. Then she drops the bomb: she has a teenage girl AND a dog. Vicky says her daughter has a lot of medical bills—*something to do with a surgery her daughter had as a baby?*—and my mother feels very connected to this single mother trying to get on her feet. She feels like the universe is trying to give her a chance to pay it forward, to help both of them. Shouldn't she do what she can for someone like this? Someone that could easily have been herself? Vicky promises to help with the housework and says her daughter will never have friends over. She assures my mother they will be very quiet, and Vicky's dog seems to get along well with our little Collie.

meant, but knowing that I wanted it in my head. I wanted to be like my sister, who was studying social justice in Santa Cruz now, working at the Resource Center for Nonviolence, living with biking hippies. I wanted to be idealistic.

I spent one night at a bar in the Mission drinking cheap beer with a boy I met in an environmental studies class. As he talked, I imagined I might work for the Sierra Club someday and come home to his passion, even though reading about rising tides and nuclear degradation was beginning to weigh on me, and I didn't understand what exactly the Sierra Club did.

The boy told me he was a registered Socialist. He was scruffy, smart, and a little oily. We talked: Marx of course, but also Owen, Saint-Simon, Nader and his inability to look not-stoned. We talked about how much we hated capitalism, and then talked about how much we doubted socialism. I smoked my first clove. I left with an ISO card and a sore throat and felt as if I had escaped complacency. I was all new.[89]

---

89 The day Vicky is supposed to move in, my mother gets a call from her bank. Vicky's check is no good and has been returned. Not because of insufficient funds, but because her account is closed. My mother is furious, because she has already turned people away and took the ad off Craigslist thinking that my wing was all rented out, and now here she is again, worrying about how she will make the mortgage payments and whether or not she is going to end up on the street. *Did she think I wouldn't find out?* My mother calls Vicky to say she can't allow her to move in. She tells her about the check and the account, and Vicky begs to meet with my mother, so she can explain.

They meet at the McDonald's across from my mother's Disney office, and when my mother walks in, Vicky is already crying. She is eating chicken nuggets and dipping them in sweet and sour sauce like it's the saddest thing in the world. Like the chicken nuggets are making things worse for her. She has on this awful pleather skirt and an animal-print tank top and my mother realizes that Vicky is not going to be turned away.

"Please, Elizabeth." Vicky keeps saying that. "It was all a mix-up with the bank. They screwed me over. I'll bring you cash, I've been trying to work this out, that out, everything out. You know how it is with a teenager, and running out of money, and Ashley's medical bills keep coming in and her father is a famous country star, I can't even tell you his name he's so famous, but maybe I can tell you later if you promise not to spread it around. He

When I came home that night, I found Travis on the couch. I was afraid he was dead, but he was only sleeping. His pants were still on, maybe they were wet, or maybe this was something I made up, something I wanted to believe. I managed him into bed while he mumbled at me incoherently, saying something about loving me. There had been a tiny pipe next to him, a pill bottle of greenery. I put it all away in a drawer of his, and crawled into bed with him, held him closely as he slept and I cried. It was the night I resolved to leave him.

When he woke up the next morning, I told him how I had found him. He didn't think much of it, and neither did I, but I wanted one of us to feel fed up. There was a new pallidity in his face, a prescience of what I would see in him months later when I visited him at the hospital. We never talked about that night, but after that I found myself in and out of periods of volatility with him, the way I had been in The House with the Red Door with my mother.[90]

I nestled next to Travis so many nights after I had told him that I didn't love him anymore. He'd say, "Should I move out?" And I told him no, I would be the one to go, when he was ready. He found an

---

won't even take my calls. I'll bring you cash tonight and will always pay on time. I'm just trying to get out of this rut." On and on while she sucks at the empty bottom of her soda cup.

90 A middle-aged guy named Chance rents the black-and-white room, the one we had painted to match the picture we found in *Martha Stewart Living*. Chance works nights at a film lab on Magnolia so she will never have to see him. He loves the house and says he is fine sharing the bathroom with Vicky and her daughter. He has his own TV so he will rarely use the living room, if at all. He is incredibly chatty on move-in day, which concerns my mother a bit, because she doesn't want to have to entertain these people, but she needs the money and figures she has already been too picky. Chance has three snakes, which is also disconcerting, but they are in an aquarium and he works nights so how could he really be much of a bother at all? He will have to sleep during the day while she's at work, then he will walk to work at four p.m. They will never even have to see each other.

apartment in the Haight, and came home to our apartment excited about his future. He said the young guys that lived in the place all smoked and painted. I didn't know where I would go.

I got a job as a cashier at a grocery store in North Beach. I thought about my grandfather often, when my back ached. I gave the socialist boy a blowjob in his dorm room one night, gagging, my mind drifting. Days later, I told him that I couldn't commit to activism, couldn't imagine a life of struggle against ideologies. I told him I wanted to write, I thought this would be a very different kind of job, and he discouraged me. I moved on to an older guy who worked at the grocery store with me. I let him come over one night because he asked so many times. Travis was in the Haight, getting to know his new roommates, marathon smoking with them. Or so I assumed. The grocery guy brought over 99 Bananas in tiny airplane bottles and I thought of my mother, how she had snuck the same sweet yeasty smelling stuff into her coffee cup. I found myself naked on the futon, drunk and kissing him, not knowing how to say no, feeling disgusting, and thinking of my mother. How much I missed being wrapped in warm towels. He tried to get inside me several times, and I couldn't get him to stop, so I went to the toilet, naked, not knowing how else to say no, and I stuck my fingers down my throat, forced myself to keep throwing up until he left.

Days before Travis left for good, we got into bed and got stoned. He motioned to hold me, and I pushed him off. "Don't," I said. "If you can't keep yourself from doing that, you should sleep in the living room."

I had wanted to refuse him, to know that I could leave, for so long.[91]

---

91 The first night Vicky and her daughter Ashley are in the house, my mother wakes up in the middle of the night to this horrible noise. She thinks a very old man is dying, or there is a sea lion in the house, but it's the stupid dog. No warning or anything. My mother panics because of her insomnia. *Once I wake up I never can get back to bed.* She tells Vicky to get the dog out of the house, but every month there is another excuse for another

problem. The dog is often an excuse for why Vicky can't pay rent. This mangy eighteen-year-old braying animal that runs into walls, and has outlandish vet bills, a dog no one in their right mind would keep alive.

Icky Vicky, as Randy calls her, never pays rent on time or in full even once. There is much arguing and negotiating all the time, then some cash thrown my mother's way. Icky tells my mother she is working as a temp for the studios, but if ever my mother comes by the house during the day, there's Vicky, watching Maury Povich on the loveseat. Vicky is somehow always between temp jobs. It takes my mother a long time to realize that most of what comes out of Icky Vicky's mouth is complete bullshit. Like with the medical bills. Vicky says she is trying to pay off her daughter's surgery. Apparently, as an infant, Ashley had to have half of her stomach removed, and some Beverly Hills plastic surgeon offered—God knows why—to fix the girl up years ago. Icky Vicky turned him down though. Of course. My mother guesses that in fact Vicky is some sort of escort or call girl.

After a few months, Vicky gives up the charade. Gets dressed up in these sleazy cougar clothes, even though she is scrawny and wrinkled, every night.

amanda MONTEI

THE ROOM NEAR LAKE MERCED

I moved out to live with some college girls I met at the grocery store, and began writing seriously. I wrote a novel about my mother, but didn't attend to it as such. I titled it *Hiding Places* because everyone in the book was hiding secrets, and then I abandoned it en masse when it finally occurred to me that I was only trying to tell her story. I didn't want to admit to myself that her stories were all I had in me, and that I was writing her away.

I often spoke to her on the phone about her childhood, the two of us piecing together similarities, doing our own genealogical connections and analyses. To my mind, my mother's brain was under water, warped by years of wanting to go back to those days in Hancock Park, that big house, that red surrey. I thought of all the coffee table books my mother had of Monet's impressionist scenes, because coffee table books, especially books about art and history, are important to have out for company. What she saw of her past seemed to be liquid and blurry, like *Water Lilies.*

During one of these conversations, she told me about the parties her parents used to throw. She said, "We had Reagan over you know."

"Reagan?" I said. "Really."

"I think we had Reagan over in those days. All the time, I think."

"Really?"

"Yes, I think so. My parents were Republicans then. Can you believe it?"

She told me stories about my sister too, but I knew many of these stories were really about me, were images of my childhood that stayed with me over the years.

"The watermelon hat was mine," I said, after she reminisced about how cute Melissa had been.

"No, you had the strawberry hat. But you *were* a grape for Halloween once. You must be confusing your fruits."

But the watermelon hat memory *is* mine. I wore it while I played with my Barbies in the hot tub at the hotel on Sea Island, when my parents were still married. My sister and I drew bikinis and ballgowns onto the dolls with colored shaving cream, just before the hurricane hit and we ran indoors. I can still see the wet green rind bobbing over the right side of my face, peripheral. It is one of my last memories of us all feeling like a family.

"Fine," I said.

I wanted to be close to her again, but whenever I corrected her she felt as if it was a punishment. I knew there was a new hardness in my voice, a resistance in my body that had begun in The House with the Red Door.

"I don't know why you think I don't know you," she said. "I really thought I would be a better mother."

I felt I should cry, but instead I shrugged my shoulders and said, "I wrote a book about you."

"God help us all," she said. "Can you tell me how it ends?"

I could have told her that pills and wine killed the mother in *Hiding Places*. I could have told her that the daughter character learned something. That because of how her mother slipped under she reformed, erased every failing in her character, every part of herself that resembled her mother. But this was why I couldn't finish the book. I knew the truth.

I said to her, "The book doesn't *end*."

"What do you write about now?" she asked.

"Other stuff," I said, but my mother didn't believe me.

"Then why do you ask me so many questions?"

"Sometimes, it's you, but it isn't *about you*."

The phone line went quiet.

"Why have you stopped writing about me?" she said.

And I said, "I haven't."[92]

---

92 After Chance has been living in the black-and-white room about a week, he comes into the kitchen one evening on the weekend, makes some food and begins chatting with my mother and Randy. My mother doesn't want him getting in the habit of being *entertained* so she takes her wine into her bedroom, hoping Randy will get the idea and stop egging Chance on. Randy doesn't get the hint, instead just stays at the yellow table gabbing with Chance until it's time for Randy and my mother to leave for dinner.

My mother goes out the front door first, and as she's walking out, she hears Chance mention—or maybe she is in the conversation when she he says it—that he's gay. He isn't really allowed visitors, and she has always loved gay men, so what does she care. Chance and Randy keep talking after she goes to the car, but when Randy finally comes out through the front door he cannot keep a straight face. He gets into the car and starts laughing and cannot stop.

He says, "The guy was just explaining to me he's bipolar! He just told me all about how many times he's been hospitalized and that his sister is actually his legal guardian because he was declared *non compus mentis*! He has to take his meds regularly and if he ever gets seriously depressed or becomes a problem we are supposed to notify her immediately! How do you attract such shit, Elizabeth, isn't your life a funny joke. Let's laugh and laugh about how fucked you are over our cheap fast food dinner date because I hate real restaurants or don't think you're worth it and then we can play all night in bed and you can wake up in the morning and find a way to care for your indigent tenants! I may be a married man with a girlfriend but my life is not nearly as fucked as yours, Elizabeth!"

Chance pays on time for about three months, then he starts to slip mentally. My mother sees him in the morning before work and he tells her he is depressed and can't sleep. She feels for him of course. Randy—who, because of his job, has to train people to work nights and sleep days— says that the worst thing for an unbalanced person is to work nights and sleep days. Chance starts taking even more meds, tries to manage his state of mind. He takes the ADHD drug that is kind of an upper. She and Randy are drinking one night at the house when Chance offers some and, *man, is it ever an upper.*

THE HOSPITAL

I found out about the hospital and Travis's head long after I left him, when I was nearly through with college. I was sleeping with someone new. The new someone and I were in my bed watching *Coffee and Cigarettes* and feeling artsy when an old friend called to tell me.

I went to the mirror in the bathroom alone, and saw that I was smiling. I knew he had gotten heavier into drugs after I left him. The guilt, coupled with a smile I couldn't control, made me wonder about myself. I used to fight with him, even when he was being good to me and I just went with it. I had this feeling, staring in the mirror, that I wanted things to be more complicated than they were. It's always how I felt with my mother, and it's always how I imagined she felt. Like I was outside myself. I think some people like to say that you do that sort of thing when you think you aren't deserving of happiness. Maybe that's true. I thought, running my hand over my lips, that maybe what's more true is that you know that happiness is something you have to create.

I didn't yet know what it was that had put him in the hospital. He had taken a lot of acid in the years we'd been together, at the parties we escaped to in the Red Door days, but I didn't think that alone could drive someone into a coma.

I thought, I shouldn't tell my mother about any of this.[93]

Travis's mother waited at the entrance to the hospital for me. They had helicoptered him into Stanford after he was found

93 On the fourth day Chance spends locked in his room, my mother calls his sister, who comes to visit and gets him back in shape. He goes back to work a few weeks later.

unconscious by one of his Haight roommates. She was sitting on a hard bench staring, her hair stiff, like a little blonde helmet made of straw, and the rows of potted hydrangeas lining the walkway hung about her tiny buckled frame. The pink petals mocking her, mocking me. Walking up to her, I was shaky and out of breath. I hadn't seen her since I left him. She's French-Canadian, very short and sweet, and I felt I had wronged her by leaving him. When I hugged her, she felt so small, like a child.

She made small talk but my answers were terse and detached. I was thinking about the pink hydrangeas and how inappropriate they seemed. I couldn't look at her. I knew she wanted to know why I had left him. I knew he never could have told her what I thought of him and how I blamed him for all of my shortcomings. How many times I had called him stupid and said that we only loved each other because we hated our parents. He would have wanted me to remain pure in her eyes, so that I could remain so in his.[94]

---

94 One night my mother has her friend Nikki over. They are drinking wine and smoking pot at the yellow table. My mother thinks about how I always hated Nikki because she is young and pretty and blonde, and my mother and Nikki go shopping together. My mother wonders whether or not I ever knew the sort of trouble they got into together. This has never occurred to her before, though just before I left home, when they started hanging out, I used to say, "You're not young anymore. You are a mother now. You can't go partying with blonde girls named Nikki, talking about sex tricks and cocaine, buying Juicy Couture shirts at Fred Segal."

They are pre-partying before a Mahjong game. They often hang out with rich Jewish ladies, women my mother knows through a friend she worked with long ago, who she recently reconnected with. They eat expensive finger foods and take little coke hits out of necklace bottles and drink all night. Before they leave, they decide it might be fun to snoop around Chance's room and check out his snakes, and his new weirder creatures. The general state of things. As soon as they open the door, my mother feels embarrassed, even through her haze. There are big glass boxes with all sorts of snakes: one above the television, one by the window, even one in the closet. Everything a mess. Not grimy, but upturned. Like he had just had a throwing fit before he left the house. And all in between the black and white stripes are pictures of naked guys, torn from magazines. Guys with huge penises, pasted all over walls. Guys posing, holding their members, staring

When we reached the ICU ward I said, "I didn't know he would ever get into that sort of thing," and then I blushed. I had violated the eye-code, and I didn't yet know what sort of thing he had gotten into. She didn't say anything in response. She seated me and walked away, assuring me she would return. There was something brazen and stoic about her detachment.[95]

---

into the camera like it's no big deal to be staring down at her from the walls of her beautiful black-and-white room. Where only years before her mother has lay sick and dying. Guys with construction hats on. In bondage gear. All of them staring at her as if to say, "Look what you got yourself into now Elizabeth, isn't this just the way life shakes down."

95 There are times when Icky Vicky and Chance sit around the yellow table with my mother and Randy and each one of them gets high, each in their own way. To my mother, they occasionally feel like some sort of strange, new family. Vicky takes some of Chance's Adderall and gets hyper and chatty. She tells stories about her days in AA, about Ashley's father the country star. My mother recounts stories about her family, about what's happening with the house. She suspects none of them care about the legal stuff, that they tune out for these conversations, but sometimes my mother feels as though Vicky understands her tug of war life.

One night my mother and Vicky are talking with Ashley, who is in her little Burbank High cheerleader uniform as always. Randy is there too. They are all at the yellow table, and of course Vicky and Ashley are flirty, have been since the minute Randy showed up. They are always running to the door with raised voices to say hi, after being quiet and sulky in the living room all day. Cooing, they give him big full-body hugs, rubbing their tits on him a little too long. He holds on a little too long himself. Certainly neither party ever has the respect for my mother to feel as though they should act with a *modicum of propriety.* "Can I do anything for you Randy? Oh Randy he's so funny and smart," they say. Though my mother suspects they are just deprived, just looking for any male attention whatsoever. Of course they also think he is a big money hot shot, working as the boss at Disney. Little do they know he sits in an editing room all day.

Vicky asks Ashley to show my mother the scars on her stomach, pulls up her daughter's little tank top and all along Ashley's waistline is this pink line, like a belly chain or the top of invisible pants, and it occurs to my mother that maybe Ashley had been given a tummy tuck by that Beverly Hills doctor. That Vicky may have been trying to cover it up, using her daughter as another excuse to avoid paying rent. My mother can't bring herself to confront Vicky about all the inconsistencies in her stories.

Hospitals are all about doors and passageways, ingresses and egresses, and I had the unsettling feeling that nothing in the place was constant, that no person or condition or activity had any foundation, that we were all just floating through these sterile, milky corridors.

His mother shared a private waiting room with another woman, whose husband had just had a heart attack. There were blankets and bags of Doritos scattered everywhere and the distinct smell of body odor and quiet nocturnal flatus brought on a familial intimacy. She told me the Doritos were the only thing that made the other woman feel better. Buried under these signs of ersatz nourishment and rest were two chairs pulled up to a counter, a long mirror hanging opposite the chairs, and some silk flowers in a cracked and frosted vase which brought a terribly broken air to the room. I pictured them sleeping there, hunched over, the woman with cheddar powder in the corners of her mouth, his mother with her immovable hair deflating, both of their palms nestled under their chins as though in prayer.

We waited for visiting hours to begin, and I spent much of that time thinking of all the worry and teardrops that had puddled and dried on that faux wood counter, and the as yet unknown emotions that would sweep through these rooms only to be buried and reconciled in the years to follow.[96]

"This is why I'm saying," Vicky says, "that you just have to learn to be more patient, Elizabeth. We're all trying, we're all struggling." So many nights my mother wonders why she has to care for these people when no one is taking care of her.

96 Randy gets to the house after work some nights before my mother has made it home, finds himself all alone with Ashley. My mother wonders, of course she wonders. Even when my mother is home, some nights Randy goes out onto the deck and looks into my old bathroom window, the bathroom all the tenants now share, while Ashley is showering. You can make out every line of her body through that frosted glass window, and it seems as though she stays in there longer, with her arms posed, holding her hair up like she is putting on a show, like she knows he's standing there.

When the nurse finally took us in to see him she said, "Are you *ready*?" I had to swallow the upset. First the pink hydrangeas, then the waiting room mirror, now the nurse. No one seemed to notice the impact each detail of this place was having on its visitors.

Travis's mother nodded, and though I didn't feel ready, I let the nurse open the door to his room. Through the Clorox air I could smell him. I breathed it in and then it was behind my eyes and I almost fell over. I couldn't complete my step forward, lost my balance and fell back.

His mother took my arm. We didn't look at each other, only at him. It was all tubes and cold and white. That awful sound of fake breathing and heart rhythms that you hear on the primetime medical shows was everywhere. They had shaved part of his head, but his face was bristly, his mouth slack. He looked brain-dead and the nurse must have sensed me thinking this because she said we wouldn't know how his brain would be affected for a few days, if he woke up at all. He was frail, looked like a kid on that bed, and I missed his mouth on me, his eyes. Those hollow yearning eyes.

There was a burn or corrosion on his arm, something raw and new. I fingered the scab, a void on his thin soft arm, and I stroked it the way he used to stroke my eyebrows, smoothing the hair out before he kissed them. Before I looked up and felt self-conscious about his mother watching me, when it was just that little dead part of his skin and me, I thought about how much my mother had loved him and I wondered if it was for the same reason that I had. Because

---

Nikki's sister falls asleep one night on my mother's bedroom floor, after too many drinks and other stuff and Randy carries her into the living room, tucks her into that little white loveseat. He pets her hair and just stands there, staring at her. My mother walks in on him, swears he is considering taking very strong advantage of the situation. She drags him out but knows she will never forget the lustful look on his face, the feeling of realizing that she does not really know this man at all. Randy says that Nikki and her friends are fun because you never know what might happen with them.

he had given me something she couldn't.[97]

As I listened to the breathing machine, I tried to remember the first time he spoke to me in high school, our first kiss, what we ate for dinner the first night in our apartment. I couldn't place any of it.

I could recall a night we spent at the yellow table when he told my mother that he had fallen in love with me when I walked by him at school and he noticed my hipbones through my jeans. I had given him one of those teenage scrapbooks for him in high school, before we drove north, when we still used words like soul mates and we thought we might live a charmed magical life. I thought of the way I had organized those images of us. There was a page I titled *Surviving Christmas* and in it there were pictures of his skinny face, squinting red eyes and big smile. He held up bagged gifts from my mother. Things she had picked up in checkout aisles all year, obvious re-

---

[97] After about six months of all this she tells Icky and Chance that she is fed up. She is paying all the utilities and cleaning up Icky's dog's shit everywhere. After this, the tenants team up on her regularly. She goes into my old wing of the house and tells them she needs the rent money, and they both start yelling about clogged drains in the bathroom. Icky has stopped paying rent altogether, but it takes three months of nonpayment to evict someone legally.

Lo and behold, Chance has an outburst at work and gets fired. He locks himself in the black-and-white room for days on end and won't come out except when Vicky is there and my mother is at work. He stops paying rent. Now, she is supporting three crazy people, none of them paying her one red cent. Hot showers, central air and heat, electricity, all paid by my mother with no way to cut off their utilities. She calls the Sheriff and he explains that she would be breaking the law if she changed the locks on them or tried to kick them out without a legal eviction.

So she waits. She files all the papers and gives full legal notice and on the very last day of the three months, they all move out. Chance has his sister come pick him up, and he gives my mother a kind of thank you letter. She knows she will never forget the look on his face as he walks out, through the red door, holding his sister's hand like a child.

gifts. There were no pictures of my mother in that album.[98]

---

98 She was good at hiding. Though I didn't visit much then, not even on holidays.

She would say it really started before Icky and Chance, carried over too. It started with her first tenant, Dave. The gun-toting drug dealer. When did he move in? Out? She always said time was hard to keep track of then. And afterwards, she buried it all. Dave was very sweet, except he also had a crazy dog, a vicious pit bull that he told my mother was a terrier before he moved in. As though she wouldn't know the difference.

After a weekend away with Randy, my mother found out there had been cops in her house because they suspected Dave of dealing. That's when she finally made him leave. When he first moved in, he always had coke and Randy wanted to party party all the time and my mother hadn't touched the stuff in twenty-five years and she was drinking of course and it just seemed like why not? And then why not again. And again.

Her old friends Bob and Jennifer asked her to come down to visit them on Independence Day, just before she broke up with Randy. They had been living in Laguna Beach since they got married, though she hadn't seen them in years. Jen had been diagnosed with cancer of the lung and heart a few years prior. It was inoperable. It spread to her throat, her larynx, but they had continued doing coke and full-on partying. Bob was still rolling in money from his father's death so many years prior. They had removed Jennifer's larynx and now she was living with one of those holes in her throat. They begged my mother to please just come visit. They had a suite on the water in Dana Point, and she thought well why not? She was worried she wouldn't be able to pay the mortgage that month and they promised there were no strings attached and she would get a free vacation. She arrived at the hotel at noon, and they showed up at nine pm with coke and a cooler full of beer. Jennifer had a bag packed with nightgowns, had the hole in her throat. And they had one of their friends there for my mother to meet. Of course, it was all a plan for a big sex party. Jennifer dressed up in her sex outfit, paraded around, sharing all the libations. She and Bob talking at the exact same time constantly, Bob holding the mic to her throat. Naturally, because of her illness everyone was patronizing her. She got in the jacuzzi, rolled around, Bob jumping to keep her throat dry, my mother eventually helping, all to keep it from getting infected. Finally, she got out. She was still so beautiful even though she was so sick. She had sex with the friend, Bob tried to make my mother watch, my mother saying Bob I am not into this I do not want to watch! They talked later and Bob agreed to loan my mother money to make a mortgage payment. He came up to The House with the Red Door and met Randy. They all shared some coke and Bob gave her nearly two thousand dollars for a mortgage payment. She was supposed to pay it back when the

I drove down to Santa Cruz to see my sister after the visit to Stanford, after first sobbing in my Volkswagen beetle in the hospital parking lot. I wept during the whole drive, and admitted to myself—and later to my sister, who held me—that I couldn't reconcile the feeling that I had pushed him into whatever addictions led him to that cold bed.

Travis and I had done the same drive to Santa Cruz together, through the windy redwood-damp highway. We had visited my sister often, had climbed trees with pipes tucked in our pockets. We had made plans for growing up while we sat in redwoods, and had imagined ourselves travelling and staying in love. The drive was long and green, my mother might say *sublime,* and I remember thinking that the world felt so open and unknown.

This is adulthood, I thought. I've finally found it.[99]

---

family estate settled. Of course that never happened.

99 When my sister came to visit for Christmas the second year I was away, my mother was deep into cocaine. Randy and my mother were staying up most nights until four in the morning, then work the next day, doing more lines and having sex in the projection room. All the employees knew there was some craziness going on between them, though they pretended to be just friends, what with work policies. My mother wanted to be alone that Christmas, didn't want to feel like a bad mother again. Melissa spent a lot of that time crying, yelling, just trying to get through to my mother.

For Randy, it was all about the hot sex and drugs and part of my mother wanted that too. She had never had a life of her own, had always been kept in the house by my father, had to take care of us girls for years alone, feeling trapped and lost without a family. She had to forget about them. She wanted to believe she could start over again. Could make mistakes and do stupid things and live her whole teenage life over again and come out on top this time. It was such a rollercoaster with Randy. One day it was happy crazy joyous sex and romance and the fireplace roaring in her room. Satin lingerie and jewelry. The next day he would go off with his kids and his wife and she was alone. *Broke lonely scared.* She finally slipped under when Icky and Chance were living in The House with the Red Door rent-free. Her car had been repossessed because she couldn't keep up, and she was riding her bike to work when her neck completely frozen. The doctor prescribed her muscle relaxers and codeine and she drank wine with the pills, took two weeks off work to heal, and it all added up.

I never went back to the hospital, but I learned weeks later from Travis's mother that he had woken up, and suffered only a short-term memory problem, like the guy in the movie who leaves Post-it reminders everywhere. I didn't believe it until the calls started. He would leave me voicemail messages, saying it had been a while and he was so glad I had come by to see him, and that he heard my voice when I was there and felt my hand on his arm and he missed me. Did I miss him? And then, minutes later, he would call again, saying it had been a while and he was so glad I had come by to see him, and that he heard my voice when I was there and felt my hand on his arm and he missed me. Did I miss him?

He was all black spots, all the time.

I wanted to mail him a Post-it note. I wanted to write on it: *You are in love.* I hoped that after he opened the envelope, he would forget that he hadn't written on the Post-it himself. I hoped that he would stick the note on his bathroom mirror or his toilet or maybe even on his pillow beside where he rested his cheek, and he would see it every morning, and each time he did, his heart would do a little two-step, and he would smile.

The doctor told his mother it was congenital: a patch of tangled arteries in his brain. Too much stress on his body had caused a rupture. I had kissed his forehead so many times, and he had run his hands through his hair when he was worried, and all the while, there had been something crouching, swelling inside him, and he had never known.

One day, she passed out in the backyard on the deck, and Icky and Ashley came home and found her there, probably thought she was dead, and that was it. They never let her forget that day. "We saved you," Icky said over and over, like they shouldn't have to pay rent because they didn't let her die. So it went on, with that stupid dog, who at night would just walk up to a wall and bray at it all night, and when Icky wasn't around my mother would think. *Should I just throw this crazy blind dog into the pool and let it die?*

PART FOUR

amanda MONTEI

THE HOUSE WITH THE RED DOOR

I made a plan to come home the year after Travis went into a coma. I missed my mother.

The day I came home everything smelled warm. Everything looked and felt like my mother's breath. Acrid and aging. I expected as much, but I couldn't help thinking of the way the house had looked in those first weeks. "A place for everything and everything in its place," she had said.

Now, dishes overflowed the sink as though they were living things, parasites attaching themselves to the counter with fork legs and spoon hands. There was peanut butter by the white loveseat, a spoon wedged inside. Sticks of butter softened on the countertop, in the butter-yellow glow of the kitchen. Snack packaging all over the yellow table. Empty chardonnay bottles. And the main event, which I knew was somewhere backstage: a mother growing slowly horizontal, her belly now a paunch, where once it was carved muscle.

The House with the Red Door was growing wayward. The house that was once a home, and had been nurtured by a mother. A mother who used to yell *five minute blitz!* every afternoon, to get her young girls excited about running around to tidy up. A mother who used to clean before the housekeeper came because *the housekeeper's job is to do the other stuff.* Who left lights on in the clean house before long vacations, so that returning would feel safe.

She was different now.

I wanted to pull my skin off. I called her name and when she didn't answer, I assumed she was sleeping through my big return. I had used up all that negative energy years ago in this house, or so I told myself. Over the next few years, I would not allow myself access to any sort of anger. I had left the cycles behind, and soon I would go away and stay away. I would never give up on life the way she had. I would be fine, I thought. Even if she never was.

Anger turned into something new. In that moment, I was hungry to clean and scrub and shine the way she used to, the way my grandmother used to. I wanted to make this ugliness go away. I could at least do that for her.

So I pulled crusted dishes from the sink, fought the smell. I thought about a roommate I had lived with briefly in the apartment near Lake Merced, after I left Travis. One of three girls I ended up with. She had lost her mother to cancer as a teenager, and carried this loss on her face. She hid in her room and played a game on her laptop that allowed her to make up a whole world of people with an incomprehensible language. She showed me how her avatars moved about a city she had created, how she could make them go on failed dates. Some days I felt so frustrated watching her fall away from the outside world that I felt something like hatred.

Now I knew: the girl had reminded me of my mother. Or was it myself? As I scrubbed, I thought *maybe this is okay*. Maybe laziness was the least my mother deserved. And maybe she deserved all the years she was taking. Maybe the problem the whole time was that no one was willing to let her mourn.

The dishes went more quickly than I expected and as I scrubbed I admired the little European homes on the windowsill, which my mother had dug out of storage. They were the worse for wear, but still had charm. Once I had collected all of the trash into a white bin, I walked onto the deck, where she was now keeping the rubbish cans. I thought I was through, that my mother would be pleased. I thought of how, when I was a little girl, I had surprised her with gifts, clean rooms, dinners cooked. I had learned from her that *the best feeling is giving*. On holidays, she had filled her closet with gifts for months, however cheap and useless.

I turned the white trash bin back up towards me and saw a furry grey and white strip, which reminded me of my mother's faux fur coat.

Last Christmas, driving home from a day of shopping, I had teased her about that coat, and she had said that for years she had begged my father to buy her *a real one*, and then, just before they divorced, he finally bought her foxes. Foxes were apparently a big mistake. She had always wanted a minx like my grandmother, a minx with one of those beautiful silk Bergdorf's labels. She had said, "Do you know what the label on mine says? Are you ready for this? Sears Fashions. *Sears Fashions*!"

We had laughed until we teared up.

I stood on the deck, looking up at the angle of sky she had been studying for so long, and I knew I would always be reminded of her stories.

Inside, I approached her bedroom door, which was open a crack. I could see her bathroom door, also open a crack. Through these narrow slits, I peered into the bathroom where we had watched my grandmother give up on her body, where I had first glimpsed my mother's shaved pubic hair, where I had found my mother vomiting, where I now saw her fleshy body lying lifelessly beside the toilet, a smudge of bright red on the wall beside her.

• • •

When you died they found you on the toilet. *I* found you on the toilet. You always said you were so close to giving up. You always said things that probably shouldn't have been said. It was what I loved best about you.[100]

---

100 Do you want to write some dialogue, mother? Do you want to write a scene? Do you want to write a poem maybe? We can put anything you want down here. You were always showing off your father's marked up books of Whitman, saying, "My father loved writing too. My father loved reading. My father loved language." You wanted so much to believe that we were capable of passing good things like a love of poetry through our blood. What could we write down here that would help you—and me—believe it? Do you want to write a joke? You're so good with jokes. You're so funny. You used to say, "My humor is the only way I survive it all." And even this was

They found you hunched over sitting on the toilet seat, the same way I found you that morning when you were drinking 99 Bananas in your coffee cup. Arms loose and hanging, but this time there was no heavy breathing, no breathing at all. You were going to the bathroom that morning when you realized you were just too tired to make it through another cup of coffee, another day at work, another night alone. You were on the toilet when you saw the pills and you took one after another after another after another, thinking how nice it would be to finally get some sleep.

You said, "If you ever have to choose, if you ever have to pick a song to play at my funeral, please play 'Somewhere Over the Rainbow.' The Hawaiian version. That is how I want to be remembered. As making it over the rainbow, and still swiveling my hips." I want only to commemorate you the right way. Maybe if I lay you down on that bathroom floor and I let the lights and uniformed men swirl around you and I write myself crying and shaking hysterically, maybe if I do this I can lay our story down, lay those years down and you can be something different. You can be someone else. It's easy to forget. You can finally lay down your hatred for the ugliness you saw in the world, for the ugliness you saw in yourself. "I hope you know how sorry I am," you say and say and say. I have always written in circles around you, but I'm writing into you now, into the ugly image you have of yourself. I'm writing with your hands pressing down on mine because in the end, I'm just a continuation of you. I'm writing you to kill off what you can't forget, and to show you that there is alchemy in the world after all, that we can remake ourselves together.[101]

---

funny to me. It made me giggle every time. Did you have laughs in those days when I was gone?

101 She would say I forgot to write: that she hates books that are hard to read like this, hates depressing books, drug memoirs, footnotes that take up too much of the page, *never did like David Foster Wallace found his stories depressing sentences too long*; that she loves description, loves nice scenic description *do more description of our homes our beautiful homes*

I worked so hard to make them beautiful for you girls; that all that aside somehow she feels surprised—*oh you do love me you actually understand me everyone should be understood by one person in their life*—that it's honest, *tell the publishers it's unflinchingly honest;* that she made amends with Richard, though they were never brother and sister again, never spoke even after they made up; that Travis stayed sad for so long and then one day fell in love again and she learned this *through Facebook of all places;* that she never did learn a new way of seeing herself, never found someone to love or to love her, only grew a bit older and found that women in Hollywood are now crass *that Anne Hathaway so manly women don't seem to know what propriety is anymore and if they're going to pay them to wear that many diamonds they shouldn't whoop their arms like men;* that she apologized for this and for that and still felt that every conversation was a failing on her part, that she was presenting herself wrong, though it was never a failing in my eyes, never anything like that, only a disconnect, and I tried writing half of this book in her voice, tried to let her speak through me, tried to inhabit all of her best storytelling habits, and it tore me in two when I realized I couldn't do it, couldn't write away her sadness, couldn't help her shake all those unattainable ideals; that she became a grandmother and *the happiness it brings makes living through the ugliness worth it;* and that all of this happened years later, because she didn't die in that house, she escaped somehow.

amanda MONTEI

TWIN TOWN

My mother didn't sleep through my homecoming. When I arrived home after the long drive down the 5, I was with a college roommate and her father, who had taken time off work to help us make the trip down. I walked in and found my mother sitting at the yellow table, wine in hand, smoking pot with Travis, who had moved back in with his mother down the street, because his memory issues prevented him from living independently. Everything was spotless and in order. She had spent days preparing the house for my return.

They both stood up when I came in, both beamed. He looked me up and down with the same eyes: those squinty red eyelids yearning. Like my mother, his face was wider, his chin doubled. He had filled out into the kind of man I could never imagine myself with, one that had been forced into many deep denials. He said, "Hi." He put out a hand.

I said hello, and my mother hugged me, and though she had warned me, her body was more doughy than I expected. I knew she must have been eating full fats. Cupcakes, cheeses, so much butter late into the night. This was her sad food. Still, I didn't want her to let go, I had missed her touch so much. But there was a *father* here, someone else's father. I told my mother she had to put everything away. She had to hurry. Travis had to leave. *A father* was coming up the walkway, and what would he think of this display? Travis ran out the backdoor with bongs and baggies in tow.

When everything was moved in and I was alone with my mother, I told her she couldn't invite Travis over ever again. She confessed that he had cooked her dinner, and had tried to kiss her. She said she loved him like a son, and it would be hard to cut him out of her life, but she would do it for me. I never saw him again, and over the next year she slowly stopped seeing him as well.

• • •

I got a job at a restaurant in the Valley, to pay my way through college, and I allowed myself to drink for the first time in years. I stopped getting high because drinking was the thing to do, and smoking only made my heart feel unstable. Towards the end of my time in San Francisco, I had fallen in love with a screenwriter. More than my mother, he was the reason I came back to Los Angeles, but after endless counts of betrayal on both sides, we ended it, and I felt free for the first time.

My mother and I drank together in the backyard while I finished up college. I was writing a lot, and after nights with her and cheap wine, I sat on the loveseat in the living room and tried to transcribe the conversations we had. Each one felt so camera ready, so unlike what a *real* mother and daughter should be discussing.

The night I traipsed down Sunset after signing a consent form for the *Real World* at Les Deux I came home to her. I was not the kind of girl that wanted that sort of *industry attention*, but in my stupor it felt bizarrely glamorous. I told her all about the three-way kiss they caught on film and *oopsy what if it's on the show*! I told her how I had taunted the cameramen, because after signing the release I was told that I couldn't treat them as though they were there, couldn't treat them as though there were people behind cameras. I looked right into the cameras and spoke to them, ruining every scene. I had also accidentally let the bidet at the real world house spray all over my slinky blue dress and my breasts had popped out while playing basketball on the recycled plastic court—the Los Angeles house was eco-conscious.

When I came home, my mother and I smoked cigarettes together on the warped deck and swelled inside like teenagers dishing.

I was finally coming into my body, learning I had the power to seduce.

"You are so lucky," she said to me that night. "I was never able to be sexy and young in Hollywood. Enjoy it while it lasts."

A video of that kiss did eventually pop up online on an MTV outtakes page, under some header like *Sluts Visit The Real World House*. I cursed this dumb notion of reality, and did not share the video with anyone, not even my mother, feeling baited and yet embarrassed by my behavior.

After graduating college, I ran off to Africa to teach English, the way young white girls do. I wanted to be far away, but I also wanted to *do something*.

My mother worried. Before I left, she said, "Make sure you remember what Africa smells like." I told her to stop *exoticizing* but I noted the smell in the Nairobi airport anyway, and thought of her whenever I caught a whiff of bush fires.

While I was away, she had a mammogram, then biopsies. She didn't tell me until I returned. She didn't want me to even consider coming home early. Her breasts were needled, and she was alone, and I was on the other side of the world enacting a savior complex while they removed bits of her body, and while she tried not to let this send her into a spiral. I would never get the whole story about these health problems out of her—it wasn't something she wanted to discuss—and I would always regret not being by her side.

I returned to The House with the Red Door with bags of *Konyagi* gin for friends, planning to stay with her for a few months while I got my bearings. A few weeks later, she drank every packet of that African gin while I was sleeping, and I moved out for good.

For a while, I had one-night stands with actors and musicians and writers with big hair, big egos. I tried not falling in love, and then I tried falling in love.

There was an actor with a girlfriend he planned to marry, a girlfriend who was living across the country. He got me into Bulleit bourbon and we read Eugene O'Neill together in bed. I promised him that all I wanted was to fuck, have fun, but I fell in love and never told him. When his girlfriend found out about us, he put an end to things. I dated a devout Christian after that, who married the girl he left me for. He told me he would take me to the south of France, where we would make babies. He would make a good girl of me and I said "Don't tease me like that!" Wanting so badly to have an uncomplicated life. Wanting so badly to be that good girl.

There was a time when I gave myself to many men, just like my mother. And even though I was no longer living with her, we met over lunch and cigarettes often, and spoke about our desire to find someone who would let us love them passionately, and without hesitation.

Later, I too spent nights sniffing powder off keys. I had a hard time imagining my mother, or anyone, needing that feeling. I hated the way I could keep dumping liquor into my body, the way I could drink until the sun rose and not even feel it. I felt like my body was a bottomless pit. The high wasn't good for me, and for this I was glad.

The longest high I had was with a man whose father had died from the addiction. He had huge nostrils and snarky humor and never once made me feel good about myself, except when he was having sex with me and looking at my body. I thought about my mother when I came to understand that he only wanted me for one thing, thought there were things she understood that I never gave her credit for.

I latched onto him, secretly hating him, until he told me that he didn't want me anymore. I stayed not for the way he fucked me, but for the way he secretly hated me too. It all felt familiar.

After another long night I found myself at a burger joint in West Hollywood, drunk and hungry. I was with a girlfriend I met at the startup magazine I was working for that summer. The online publication had what I called then a Diet Feminism outlook, so neither of us worked there much longer. We were complaining about how all of our articles had to sound like pop songs, catchy and effervescent. The tagline at the time was *Smart, Sexy, Savvy!* and I thought this was just so much for women to live up to. What if we couldn't do all of that? A woman who had studied Business at USC, who had soft skin and long thick hair, founded the company. She had definitely been a sparkly bubble girl in Texas, where she grew up. She had achieved fame after a short run on the TV show *Survivor.*

When my girlfriend and I walked into Astro Burger on Santa Monica we saw that the wicked husband from *Titanic* in line, ordering a turkey burger and fries. We heard him say *pickles* and we melted. We sidled up next to him, and invited him back to my friend's place for *drinks and who knows what else*. He was bald and handsome and we thought he would be such a conquest.

"My mother used to be your agent," I blurted out. He asked her name, and shrunk away from us when I told him.

"I remember her very well," he said.

He apologized, saying we were too young. He left alone.

My mother and Big Melissa began speaking again. Their older sister had been having health problems, and the legal battle was nearly wrapped up. Randy had gone back to his wife. The coke went with him but so did my mother's job at Disney, when she was caught having sex with him on the job. Her nights were now wine and buttered crackers.

My cousin, Big Melissa's daughter, came to town months later. We took a late night taxi to see one of my mother's old comedians, who had become a family friend. He directed us to a party at an excessively large house in the Valley, which belonged to a famous Mexican comedian. As we sipped champagne my cousin told me her mother was also drinking too much. Big Melissa was thinking about AA. Our toes flicked the surface of the turquoise pool. There were two women with fake breasts giggling across from us. I hadn't seen my cousin since we were kids. She said she didn't understand all that had happened between our families, that her mother had never discussed the legal stuff until recently, and even now told her very little about what had happened. I lied, said I didn't know anything either.

She said, "I think AA is good for them, but it's not for me." I called her *my almost twin*, seeing my own movements in her lanky body, hearing my dry humor coming out of her. We acted as though we had escaped our mothers' influence, but on some level I knew we were both sharing our fears.

The comedian was much older than us, pockmarked and married, though still funny. I kissed him that night for too long, let him feel me up just enough to make me wonder in the morning whether my mother's patterns were written on me.

"Don't tell your mother," he had said. I knew I wouldn't.[102]

• • •

It was a drive like any other, except her bags were packed. The color in the sky had not yet turned, it was blue and grim and I wished I

---

102 *I read somewhere that intuition isn't divine. That it's actually a result of all the people and objects we've encountered in our lives. I think that must be true to some extent, but I also think that sometimes you can just know something. It seems to me that must have something to do with God or some greater force. That's something I can leave you with. That's how I felt the day I knew I had to give it up, and must have been how my father felt when he decided he would never touch another drop. I was standing on the deck, talking to my twin sister. We had begun speaking again by that point, since all of the housing and estate stuff was nearly resolved. It was twilight, my favorite time of day, and I looked up at the sky and knew I had seen this angle of the sky so many fucking times. The purple glow wasn't even beautiful anymore. My sister was telling me about all of her problems, the way I always did with her. I could tell by the way she pronounced words that she had been drinking, and I realized I was hearing my own voice. I knew then that drinking was the only thing I cared about in the world, and knew I had to get sober or I would die standing on that deck all alone.* [redacted] *And that was it. I hated what I had become. I knew couldn't live like that anymore.*

were asleep.

"You brought slippers?" I said.

"You don't think I should have?"

"I don't think you're going to need slippers and a robe. Are you thinking of this month as some sort of vacation? You do understand that this won't be *fun,* right?"

"Do you think I need you to remind me?"

"But slippers?"

"Better to be safe than sorry."

I was still living in Los Angeles, but had long since moved out of her house. She had a new job that she hated, and was struggling to make mortgage payments. She knew these thirty days would put her over the edge financially, but she said that something had clicked, and now getting sober was all that mattered. Late one night, she had done something—something she wouldn't share with me for years—that woke her up.

Her hair was unbrushed, and cigarette ash flew in and out our windows, our throats scratchy in the moist morning air. We both smoked too many cigarettes. It had become our common ground, something we could share. We drove through the Sepulveda Pass pre-rush hour and it felt as though the hills around us were narrowing, as though we were driving underground. Everything around us was shrinking, graying, growing wet. I had this idea when I dropped her off that the turmoil, the push and pull of bad and good days, would end.

Off the freeway, the streets were dirty and empty and we drove past the place without knowing it. We drove down Pico, down down underground and under the Pacific.

"Burger King," she said, pointing. "It would be nice to get something. I don't know when they're going to feed me. Or what."

I told her we didn't have time, we didn't know how long the line would be. I told her she had to get healthy. Talked about trans fats and hormones. Body upkeep. She was much heavier now. Late nights had turned the paunch she had when I came back to Los Angeles into a general roundness. I was trying to change everything about her all at once, lecturing this way.

"We're not stopping," I said.

The woman on the phone had told her to get there early for a spot in line. If you can get here in the morning, she told her, we can get you a bed. I had imagined the endless line outside of Glide in the Tenderloin, where hungry people stood waiting all afternoon for food, for a bed. I used to walk by that line on my way to the MUNI and imagine my mother in the line.

Days before this drive, we had met for lunch, and she brought me a pamphlet for a utopian Florida treatment center she found after calling *411* and asking for a rehab facility. Through that whole meal, she was shaking more than I had ever seen, barely able to hold her fork. As she picked at her food, she kept saying, "I just *have* to do this."

Her dream of palm trees and tennis games, massages and yoga on the beach, personalized detox meals, were now supplanted by visions of stained concrete, mornings bathed in cigarette smoke. Sobriety had become very unappealing when she found out that with her poor insurance plan the only option was a state-run facility. She was resolute about inpatient treatment, though, felt that being in a locked-down environment was the only way.

"I should at least stop at an ATM," she said.

"What are you going to need money for in there?"

"I don't *know,* sweetie. I don't know *what* to expect. I'm sure I'll need money for *something.*"

We stopped at a liquor store with an ATM and she didn't want to go in, didn't want to be tempted. I told her she wasn't going to be able to buy a bottle of Chardonnay and walk into the place with it. She laughed and patted my leg, and I must have looked away. After the ATM, we drove back the way we came, climbing up Pico, our eyes darting around. The place was a storefront like any other, with a dilapidated sign that said *Clare Foundation.* There was no line, no crowded beacon for the drunk and high. The sidewalk was desolate.

It was something like a moan, the sound she made as I parked.

Like a child's belly whine just before an outburst. Tremors overwhelmed her body. She had been to the doctors before the final arbitration in Orange County, asked if there was a pill that could put an end to her shakes. They told her it was hereditary, and prescribed her a beta-blocker. She hadn't taken her new medicine that morning, wanting to be free of everything.

"Oh, God it's just *awful*," she said.

We went in but didn't bring her bags with us. Not yet.

Inside there were young women with stringy hair and printed pajama pants and plush animal slippers. "Is this where I check in?" My mother spoke eloquently, professionally. I busied myself, studying AA and NA and CA and MA pamphlets like *Having Fun in Recovery*. I collected fliers for sober rock concerts.

When my mother was done checking in, we walked back to my car, sat on the cold leather and closed the doors. We smoked more cigarettes. She was to go back in a half hour and begin admittance paperwork.

"They're all *homeless*," she whispered. "They're all *crack heads*."

We drove in circles.

We parked next to Burger King. I was beginning to agree with her. She didn't belong with these people. She was much better off, and it seemed almost silly for her to take a bed from someone who might need it more. I couldn't figure out who we were, what we were doing here.

"My mother would be horrified," she said. "We're in the D.A.R. for God's sake."

I told her I didn't want to stay while she did the paperwork.

"You're just going to *leave* me there?" she said.

Her head shook from side to side. I wanted to hold it still for her. Her hands were vibrating like bird wings.

She paced the asphalt parking lot, smoked three cigarettes, relighting each a dozen times as they went out, her teeth chattering. I called my sister, who had no answers either. None of us knew the right thing to do.

My mother came back to the car resolved, and said, "I *have* to go. It's my only choice. What other *choice* do I have?"

I watched the cigarette burn out in her hand.

"Get in the car," I said. "We're going home."

• • •

I used to dream that I was climbing up my family tree, meeting everyone in my waspy, eugenics-obsessed ancestry. Each ancestor looked like they were becoming a part of the tree. A rooted pile of greening bodies.

Months after the drive, I signed up for one of those websites where you can build your family tree. I found digital images of yellowed census records, which were supposed to tell me where I came from. I found a military record that listed a great-great-someone as a Civil War lieutenant. I read a boring letter by an ancestor who apparently hated Baptists because he was a Methodist. Ironically, there is a Baptist church in Virginia founded by an eighteenth-century ancestor of mine. What was all this to me? I did not even believe the pixelated tree I ended up with. It was all too hands-off, the way the website spoke to me and guided me with search engines and scribbled death records. I went back back back but I never found Oliver Ellsworth and I never found Aaron Burr. Were these men even related?

There was a user on the website who named his family tree *how we got here*. This user popped up when I found the image of the plaque that is hammered above the doorway to that Baptist church, the one with my ancestor's name on it. *How we got here* shared my blood, and must have stared at this image the way I did, looking for some understanding in the knowledge that he was born of someone who was born of someone who was born of someone who founded a Baptist church.

Aaron Burr's grandfather was Jonathan Edwards. They were in fact related. I had wanted so long to make sense of my tangled ancestry, but when I stumbled on this information on what appeared to be a rarely visited website, I felt no great awakening.

Because I spent years researching details about my family and my mother's stories, I also found out that the barrel under a St. Bernard's neck does not carry ghosts, but it is bound up in legend. Some argue that a child once drew a picture of his St. Bernard with a barrel, and his older brother, who was a famous artist, copied this feature. The image proliferated. Others insist that St. Bernards did in fact carry spirits to weary or lost travelers in the Swiss Alps. Who knows which story is true.

I searched for all that stuff we sold, too. I wanted so badly to run my fingers along that four-poster bed that was used in *Maverick,* just one more time. I wanted to sit with Spencer Tracy and my grandmother's pony, play 1-800-DENTIST under the Babs poster again. I still imagine lining up all the places we lived in on the yellow table, each one tiny and shrunken to doll-size like the European homes my mother once collected.

After the drive to the Clare Foundation, my mother never drank again. She called her insurance company and found an outpatient treatment center in Valley Village called Twin Town. The name, she thought, was a sign.

"It's like I've come full circle," she said. "Life is so strange that way, isn't it?"

Somehow, Twin Town worked. She started carrying sobriety chips around on her keychain, and every time someone wronged her in public or at work she said, "Well, I'm pretty sure he has a drinking problem he hasn't yet dealt with." This was her new lens. Over the next year, she slowly made amends with everyone, even those she felt had wronged her, including her brother.

I tried everything to avoid family day at Twin Town. I didn't want to admit that I had anything left to *deal with,* even though she had been sober for six months.

"There's story material for you at these meetings," she told me devilishly. She had begun accruing the secrets of celebrities she met at AA, but refused to tell me them. "If you come and take notes, I won't tell anyone."

Family day was held during a regular meeting time, so there were anxious and lonely newcomers there too. My sister and I were quiet through most of the meeting. Towards the end, the group leader asked us to speak. My mother said she was thankful for her daughters, her health, her sobriety. We admitted that we felt now that our mother was watching us, waiting for us to turn into her.

The group leader said, "Are *you* afraid of becoming your mother?"

We both said, "Of course."

My mother and I smoked cigarettes together on the break, my sister standing beside us. I said I had wanted so badly to believe that those days were just days, that everyone made mistakes sometimes, but now I realized that the time we spent in The House with the Red Door was much more in my mother's eyes. My sister recounted the way our phone calls had sounded to her, when I called her as my mother and I fought. She said she dreaded hearing her phone ring in the evenings. We all agreed it felt good to talk, to put our foggy memories into words.

That night, after my mother went to bed, I told my sister about the baby and the abortion. The talk I had with my mother so long ago, in the bathroom in The Brown Condo. Melissa and I were sitting cross-legged on the too-small white loveseat, drinking wine that we had snuck into the house. I had always been told that my mother kept the baby a secret from her.

"That's crazy," Melissa said. She had known about the pregnancy before my mother did anything, she said. Before my mother decided to have an abortion. Melissa said she cried and begged my mother to keep the baby. "I wrote her a letter telling her that I would help her, that I was already helping her with you. It was completely irrational on my part, I must have been twelve."

I told Melissa that I might have made the whole thing up, my being my mother's confidante. I couldn't really be sure anymore. I had come to accept certain lies and misrememberings as fact.

"Do you remember her gold shoes?" I said. "How much I used to love them?"

"I can still picture you walking around in them," she said

We shared our fears that something lies dormant in our blood, in our DNA. Fears that a hollow spot will present itself, that we might lose ourselves the way our mother did. Not just fears of addiction, or behavior patterns, but fears that there might not be a way to find happiness in this world. I remembered my mother saying that fear is the driving force behind everything bad in our lives, and in the next few years, I would begin to whether my grandmother had taught us all that worth could be passed down for generations, and in doing so, had taught us that emptiness could be passed down too. I would cling to the details of my mother's life, and the idea that she had been born whole, that the people and things around her had made her without insides.

My mother has always had a way of dramatizing things, of making everything swell big inside her. A sweet and fatty dessert: a way to mend a broken family. A ruined dessert: a family that can never be healed. When I went to sleep that night, I had a dream, one that I would continue to have, in various derivations, over the next few years: I found a word that defined my mother, and when I found the word I understood her. I could fit her into that word and that word could map itself on her and that was all I needed. And then I found a word that defined the way I understood my mother, the exact degree to which I knew myself to be a part of her, and to which I knew she was a part of me. And then I was searching my mother's body. She was whimpering, but not loudly. She didn't want to be heard, because we were hiding. The search was not frantic, but calculated, soft. My fingers spreading folds of skin, pulling her arms and legs up and over her head. There was blood on the carpet below us, puddling.

She said, "What is it?"

And I said, "I don't know. Are you sure it's coming from you?"

She whimpered a bit more, and said she could feel her body burning all over. Feeling that if I stayed, I too would be contaminated, I left her there, her body still seeping blood. I went somewhere, I don't know where, but I knew it was not where I began.

A year after my mother got sober I had to go to another event, this time at her local AA meeting, where she had been going weekly since her outpatient services at Twin Town had ended. It was in a run-down church hall. They gave her a cake. That's what they called the event: *getting your cake.*

After she blew out the candles, my mother gave a little speech, though I don't think one was required. She apologized to her sister, who had flown in from Florida for the cake, and then she addressed me.

She said, "[redacted]"[103]

After the cake ceremony I made jokes with the AA people. I told them I was a writer and they asked me if I wanted to join them. They thought this was very funny and so did I. I told them I probably would someday, and they laughed even harder.

I don't know how I will end up. This is not a conversion story, though sometimes I wonder if it might be better if it was.

• • •

The family compromised. She got to keep the house, but was written out of the estate. When everything was settled and signed, her lawyer mailed her a bill. She had to sell the house to pay the legal fees that she had accrued over eight long years.

"They won anyway," she said to me on the phone.

---

103 I have given enough of you away already.

She quit her job, sold nearly all of her things at a garage sale, and prepared to move out of Los Angeles for good. She would relocate to an apartment in the Bay Area, where my newly married sister was expecting her first baby. She would leave Hollywood behind, leave this *fucked up town* and get a job that she enjoyed.

The day before she left, we sat on lawn chairs in front of The House with the Red Door, as movers packed up her things. "This house is haunted anyway," I said.

She handed me an envelope. Inside were all of the profits she had made off the things she had sold. She put her chin down, tried to keep herself from shaking.

"I've never loved anything more than my girls," she said. "Please fall in love with *something*."

After she moved, she took up cooking, with so much time to fill. For her first sober Christmas, she cooked Cornish game hens. We sat at a card-table nestled between her small kitchen and small living room. Next to our plates were gold napkins in seashell napkin holders, computer paper folded in half to stand up, our names written in calligraphy. Melissa and I wrestled hen bones, trying to hide how absurd the meal felt to us. My grandmother's silver, which my mother had laid out, was of no use. Still, I was happy that even though she was buttering her hen, the dinner was not all sad food. There was a bit of harmless loveliness in the way she had cooked for us.

I speak to her on the phone now, but I listen differently than I did in my college years. Her meals of choice color her now. She tells me on the phone that she is making sage butter. Food is a container for her that when done right, carries all the dreams of class and propriety she grew up with. Her taste is her, plated. Her food speaks to me now. She guards her real worries, and I withhold my criticisms of our history of privilege, both of us knowing we will never quite understand each other again. It is not rare to hear she is eating sad food, but there are also salads made with garden vegetables, berries from the farmer's market, aged balsamic. She takes up jogging for the week, and reads self-help books. During these periods, I wonder if we might find happiness after all. When I visit her, she walks naked around her rented apartment, the bathroom wafting scents of fancy lavender soaps. Her hips lined now with cellulite, tick marks of years and lost possibilities.

Her body is all age now, all letting go.

On that first sober Christmas, my mother pulled a box of old pictures out of a storage closet and we looked through them together. I let her tell me her stories, even if she had told me them before. She knew I was writing about her again.

She told me about finding a Facebook page with pictures of old Hollywood. We pulled it up on the computer. She showed me a picture of Cave de Roy on Sunset Plaza, where my grandfather was a private member. She showed me a picture of Ciros restaurant, Abbie Lane standing in front, next to a blue Jaguar.

"My parents had their own table there too, right about this time," she said. "They had the same car." She pointed to a man in the back of the picture. "That may be my father!"

The man in the picture didn't look like my grandfather, but I didn't correct her. I let myself believe, for that night, that my grandparents had spent that night chatting with Abbie Lane, and that they had never forgotten it.

We found a collection of slides that night, images from her childhood, the good days in The Big Brick French Normandy in Hancock Park. Holding one of the slides up to the light, I saw my grandfather standing by a lake, a cigarette hanging from his lips, his shirt unbuttoned. My mother took him to the lamp, looked more closely. We both thought he looked very handsome. A carved chest, a knowing smile.

"This is not how I knew him," she said. In his eyes was something like love. "My mother must have taken this picture."

I asked her about the picture my father has of her, on Rue de

Rivoli with the pigeons and the petit point bag. *Elizabeth in Paris* scribbled on the back. She said the picture was not of her, that it was of my father's mother, who is also named Elizabeth.

"Didn't you two go to France when you were married?" I said.

"Yes," she said. "But I never would have done that with the birds. Your father and I were always fighting on those trips. And why would I have my *needlepoint* with me in *France*? Are you kidding?"

"I think you do it better than I do," I said. "I think you tell all your stories better."

"THE END."

AUTHOR'S MOTHER'S NOTE

The author's mother wishes to make clear that certain scenes and details in this book are not as accurate as she would have hoped. Part of this, the author's mother admits, is due to her own failure of memory. When pressed by the author, certain aspects of her life simply didn't fit historical "truths," and she was forced to reconstruct her past from what she could be certain of. The author wishes to make clear that a good portion of her mother's memory appears to be an amalgamation of era-specific ambiences and vague memories. So truth is a funny thing. Nevertheless, given that, of all the twists and turns the author's mother's life has taken, the least expected, by far, has been to see that life flayed open for the world to see at the hand of her precious daughter, the author has agreed to allow her mother a few parting thoughts. The following is a list of the author's mother's minor but nonetheless noteworthy objections, which the author chose to respectfully ignore:

Page 11: Though the topic became the source of much debate between the author and her mother, the author's mother must assure those readers unfamiliar with the television show that Cosmo Topper was not callous. He was simply befuddled.

Page 14: It should be noted for those readers of the author's mother's generation that even Richard Widmark, one of the most famous film actors of the '30s, '40s, and '50s, was one of the author's mother's parent's best friends, and was in fact in their wedding party. He had been the author's mother's father's roommate in college. He too often visited The Big Brick French Normandy and they all called him "Wid."

Page 19: Bernie died at City of Hope, in the manner described, but the author's mother wishes it to be known that she was not by her friend's side, although she has always regretted that she was not. Though the author's mother did move to L.A. to be near Bernie, she only visited the hospital. Not even as much as she could have. The weight of death and illness kept her away. It pains the author's mother to think that this misremembering on the author's part might offend Bernie's friends and husband. Some things in life simply can't be rewritten.

Page 42: The sisters actually recalled this moment together as teenagers, but for whatever reason the author felt it more fitting to place this remembrance in the condo, a glass of wine in hand. The author's mother was actually okay with this, since she fondly remembers relishing many nights alone with Tori and Merlot. And of course, she thought of her sister often, in so many ways, as she always had throughout her life, the two of them separated by distance and time and so many difficult misunderstandings, but never really apart in their bodies.

Pages 68-69: The visit to Dixie's home in fact occurred one year before the author's mother's father died. Time was compressed by the author in this section, and the financial history was simplified a bit for readability. It seems important to point out this particular instance of creative license, although the author's mother finds it difficult to straighten out the timeline of her *crazy long life*, so she very much understands the need for simplification. She only wishes she could have simplified it all as she was experiencing it!

Page 81: After much thought, it was decided that *Jonathan Livingston Seagull* was in fact the book the author's mother was reading when she ran away from home in 1971. The author thought that, given her mother's class struggles, *Rich Man, Poor Man* (which naturally the author's mother also read) had richer allegorical potential.

Page 114: Clooney *never* hung out at the Laugh Factory, though there were plenty of other famous faces. If the author's mother had ever seen Clooney anywhere in Hollywood she would have cornered him in a bathroom and made love to him right then and there.

Page 175: Jennifer died right about when the house sold. Bob is in a more peaceful place now. The author's mother gave him an amends and he was very understanding. They are on very good terms now, though of course, as with everyone she has known in her life, who knows what will happen after the release of this book. She has never been able to afford to pay back her loan.

Page 203: After some very real scares with homelessness—which included facing the fact that as an old woman she may have to work the rest of her life as a greeter at Wal-Mart, and that no one in this country values the work of an aging woman who left Hollywood of her own accord—the author's mother transitioned into a quiet, ordinary life. She remained sober during this whole terrifying process, even though many nights she lay awake crying, regretful about where life had taken her, and terrified about where it might still go. She joined the ranks of wage labor, makes an *extremely* modest living now, and will probably never be able to afford to retire, but what does any of that matter. Her three young grandchildren really were the denouement, and she is alive, and she is healthy, and that is so much more than many others can say, and for that she is thankful every day.

ABOUT THE AUTHOR

Amanda Montei holds an MFA from California Institute of the Arts and is a PhD candidate and Presidential Fellow in the Poetics Program at SUNY Buffalo. Her critical writing has appeared in *Gurlesque: A Critical Anthology* (Saturnalia, 2016), *Performing Ethos: An International Journal of Ethics in Theatre & Performance, PAJ: A Journal of Performance and Art, American Book Review, Harriet: The Blog, Ms. Magazine, HTMLGIANT,* and others. Her poetry and fiction has appeared in *Dusie, Atlas Review, Everyday Genius, Coconut, Gigantic, Joyland, Pinwheel, Explosion Proof Magazine, Delirious Hem* and others. She coedits Bon Aire Projects, and edits the literary journal *P-QUEUE.* Montei is co-author, with Jon Rutzmoser, of *DINNER POEMS* (Bon Aire Projects, 2013), and author of the chapbook *The Failure Age* (Bloof Books, 2014).

www.ingramcontent.com/pod-product-compliance
Lightning Source LLC
Chambersburg PA
CBHW020155090426
42734CB00008B/828
9781937543921